Awakening Your Psychic Power ~

A Medium's Guide

Arlene Michel Rich

2015

Publishing Division of The Spiritual Awakening, LLC

Also By Arlene Michel Rich

Memoir of a Medium ~

A Bridge to the Other Side

2013

Publishing Division of The Spiritual Awakening, LLC

Dedication

This book is dedicated to my grandmother, Margaret Cannon Michel, a.k.a. Grandma Michel who taught me how natural and easy it is to communicate with Loved Ones in Spirit. She taught me by example unconditional Love and what being of service is and how we are ALL ONE!

Although she was only 4'11" she left some mighty big shoes to fill and I will be eternally grateful to her.

And she still gives the best hugs!

I also dedicate this book to my parents, Rosemary O'Donnell Michel and Robert Joseph Michel. They both crossed over to the Other Side in 2001 four months apart. One of the first things my mom said to me was that she was sorry for teasing me all those years about talking to "dead people". I am so grateful to feel their love and have them also as my helpers in the Spirit world.

Photo is of Grandma and me at the beach in

Far Rockaway when I was 4 years old.

Acknowledgements

To my Writing Coach and friend Laura. J. Kendall. You have been so helpful and supportive with this and my first book. Thank you!

To my Editor and friend Orielan Harrington. Thank you for all the hours of rewrite and suggestions. You did a wonderful job, once again.

To my Photographer and friend, Sue Kenney. You worked your magic with this cover photo as well as my first book. Thank you.

To my husband Jim who has always been my support system even when he didn't always understand my path. His love, his strength of character, intelligence and sense of humor have been the key for me to unlock who I'm meant to be! I am truly Blessed to be his partner in this life!

~and~

To my family and friends who keep me grounded when I need to be and help me fly when I need to soar.   *~and~*

To all my Spiritual teachers, my students and my clients, I thank you for being a part of my beautiful Spiritual tapestry. Thank you to all those in Spirit who have allowed me to be their voice from the Other Side. I humbly will continue to do so and for this I AM so Grateful!

Awakening Your Psychic Power

A Medium's Guide

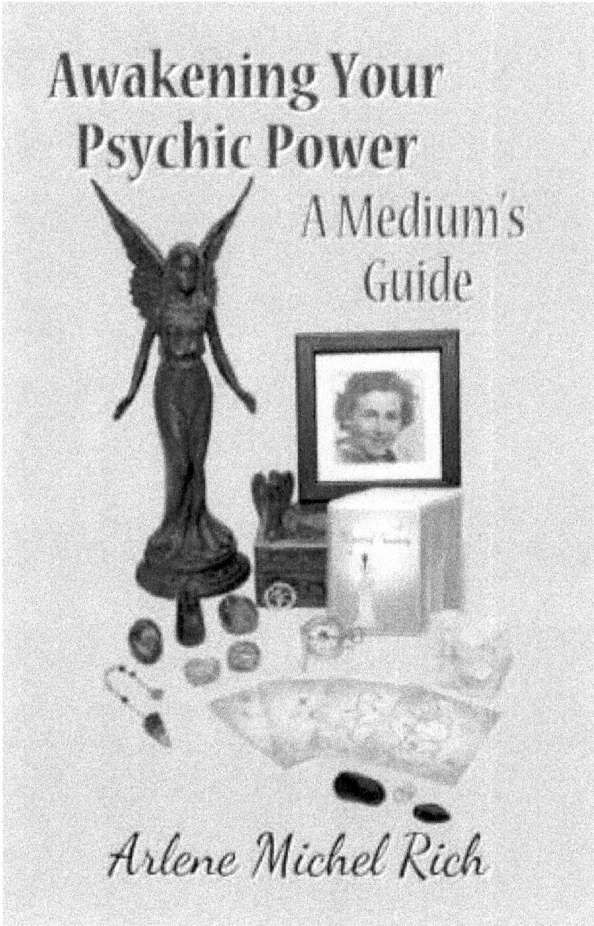

By Arlene Michel Rich

TABLE OF CONTENTS

INTRODUCTION

In my book *Memoir of a Medium - A Bridge to the Other Side* I tell how I have been talking with the Spirit world since age nine. Through the years I have learned that those we love are never far from us - both the two-legged and four-legged kind. I want you to know that you can communicate with your loved ones as well. I shared with you my real life sessions and experiences with those on the Other Side. Through *Memoir of a Medium - A Bridge to the Other Side* you are given assurances that the connection with your loved ones never dies. A book about my life as a Spiritual Medium wouldn't be complete without teaching you some practical techniques, which is why I chose to follow it up with this book.

CHAPTER 1
GROUND AND SHIELD

Before I begin any psychic or spiritual Medium work I ALWAYS surround myself in a bubble of protection by saying a prayer called the White Light Prayer of Protection.

This prayer has been used as a spiritual protection technique for around two centuries. It is the best way to protect ourselves during any kind of psychic or spiritual endeavor. It can be used for protection from the influence of anything or anyone negative. Have you felt drained when speaking to someone? Metaphysicians refer to them as psychic vampires. A good side effect of saying this prayer daily, is that it aids in the raising of our vibrations, enabling us to develop our psychic skills. Using this protection prayer each day will surround us in a pure white aura of God's protective light. We are surrounded totally in this light and protected from negative energies.

Before I get out of bed in the morning I start each day saying the White Light Prayer as well as my own prayer: "God bless me and keep me safe and may I have a great day and may I be of service to others. For this I am so grateful, Amen." ~Arlene

If, for some reason, I have forgotten to say it first thing in the morning and I have an immediate need to feel protected I say my own version: "Shields Up!"

As you begin to awaken your senses, a new fascinating world opens up to you. Your senses become heightened and you perceive them in color. There are numerous energy bodies around the human body which are: the ethereal body, the emotional body (astral), the mental body and the spiritual body. Each energy body has its own vibration frequency, from the lowest (ethereal) to the highest (spiritual). Additionally, there is a complex energy system of energy bodies known as the chakras (energy centers) and nadis (energy channels). Chakra is a Sanskrit word meaning, "wheel." Nadi is a Sanskrit word meaning "pipe" or "vein." These channels transport prana, or vital energy, throughout the human being's energy system. Traditional teachings tell us there are over 88,000 chakras in the human body. Most are extremely small and play a minor role in your energy system. There are approximately forty secondary chakras that are of significance; these are located in your spleen, the back of your neck, the palms of your hands and the soles of your feet. However, for most of us knowing the seven major chakras will be enough. These seven major Chakras run along a horizontal line, from the top of your head to the base of your spine. When I ask you to say the white light prayer I will be talking about or referring to our chakras. I thought it best to give you some information here so you are aware of where each chakra is located in your body and what it correlates to.

Major Chakras:

1.   The **root/base chakra** is associated with the Earth, with the sense of smell, and the color red. It is connected to one's relationship to money. It is located at the base of the spine and controls the pelvic area, sex organs, potency and fluid functions. The root chakra correlates closely to the reproductive organs.

2.   The **sacral chakra** is associated with water, with the sense of taste, and the color orange. It is connected to one's sexuality and enjoyment. It is located just below the navel. The adrenal glands closely correlate to the sacral chakra. It controls all solid parts of the body: the spinal column, bones, teeth, and nails, and also the blood and building of cells, kidneys, and bladder.

3. The **solar plexus chakra** is associated with fire, with the sense of sight, and the color   . It is the center of being in your power. It closely correlates to the pancreas. It controls the liver, digestive system, stomach, spleen, gall bladder, muscles, autonomic nervous system, and lower back.

4. The **heart chakra** is associated with air, with the sense of touch, and the color green. It is the center of giving, to yourself and to others. It correlates to the thymus gland and controls the heart, blood circulation, the immune system, lower lungs, rib cage, skin, upper back, and hands.

5. The **throat chakra** is associated with ether, with the sense of hearing, and the color blue. It is connected to inhibitions while speaking, fears of self-expression and being your true self. This chakra correlates to the thyroid gland and controls the jaw, neck, voice, airways, upper lungs, neck, and arms.

6. The **third-eye chakra** is associated with light and the color indigo. It is connected to trusting your intuition. The third eye chakra is located in the center of the brow and correlates to the pituitary gland. It controls the

endocrine system, left brain hemisphere, left eye, nose, ears, sinuses, and parts of the nervous system.

7.   The **crown chakra** is associated with thought and with the color violet or white. It is the chakra for connecting with Spirit. The crown chakra is located above the crown of the head and correlates to the pineal gland. It controls the cerebrum, right brain hemisphere, central nervous system, and right eye.

Exercise 1: Saying the White Light Prayer

Ask God to surround you in His white light of love and protection. With your eyes either closed or open (whichever is your own personal preference) take deep slow breaths. In through the nose with your mouth closed. Making each breath out through the mouth longer than the one before, this helps you to center and ground yourself. See or feel your crown chakra opening. Feel the energy from this white light entering your crown chakra and slowly filling your mind and body with its light and warmth. Feel it flowing throughout your entire body, filling you. Sense any dark spots in your chakras and body, focus the white light on them, until they are totally cleared.

When you are filled with this light and warmth, visualize your solar plexus chakra (just above your belly button), see, feel and sense the white light slowly coming out of this chakra. See it covering your entire body, encasing it like a protective bubble. This is God's light energy and it will protect you from anything or anyone who is negative, that you may encounter throughout your day. In my mind's eye I visualize this beautiful protective bubble completely encapsulating my body and extending arm's length out in all directions.

Remembering always to picture my back well-protected too!

The prayer is: *I surround myself with the white light of truth. Nothing but that which is of the truth and for my highest good shall approach me, for I am a child of God and God will protect me. Amen.*

I repeat! This prayer must be said before any psychic or Medium or healing work is done. It is possible that by not saying this prayer of protection (or one very similar that you personally use for the same purpose), negative energy can come through instead of only positive energies. So ALWAYS start by saying this prayer and enjoy an inner peace, knowing that you are protected. You can say this prayer at any time, no matter what you are doing and it will help to give you the benefit of both inner peace and protection.

First and foremost, rule #1 when doing psychic work is TRUST your intuition. Listen to that voice inside you. Follow your heart, gut, instincts and intuition. This can help with both your business and personal life.

Most people I speak with are familiar with their sense of intuition, or inner guidance. We all occasionally receive some inner guidance – sometimes we listen and follow the guidance, and are really glad that we did. Other times we doubt it, our logical minds question it, and we ignore it – only to kick ourselves later for NOT having listened!

The Angels tell me this is all part of the process of learning to trust the guidance you receive. Your outer reality is communicating to you all the time! Your outer world communicates what's going on inside you as a reflection and extension of your consciousness. From a metaphysical perspective, your reality is what you either create or allow (consciously or unconsciously) through your beliefs, choices, thoughts, feelings and imagination.

 Your reality serves as a gateway through which you can receive insights from the universe and your Higher Self via signs, signals and occurrences in your day-to-day life. To guide you. The more you recognize that you are connected to an infinite intelligence as you connect to Source (I choose to call God), the more you will discover the synchronicities and blessings that are all around you. A synchronicity is a situation in which separate events seem connected; a situation in which two or more things happen at the same time and seem to be connected even if they are not. Nothing is "by chance." There are never any coincidences! Or, as I say, "there are no co-inky dinks EVER!" This is my belief that has always served me well.

Here are some things I have taught my students over the years:

1. **Raise your Vibration!** The higher your vibration, the more you experience synchronicities and receive magical blessings!

How do you raise your vibration? There are numerous ways to do so on the physical, mental, emotional and spiritual levels.

Love is the highest vibration in the universe; love for you, others and your world will ALWAYS raise your vibration. And gratitude can help open your heart to more of that love. Keep a gratitude journal. I like to list five things daily I'm grateful for.

Essentially, the happier you are, the more aligned you are with your true nature and Source (God), and the more open you are to synchronicities and blessings! One powerful way to raise your vibration is to work energetically in love and light. Even or especially when we have someone in our life that has hurt us, when you think of them send them love and surround them in God's healing light. I didn't say it's easy but it is Divinely Right!

2. **Believe in synchronicities!** Another way to increase synchronicities in your life is to believe in them more, and keep your eye out for them! Understanding that everything is energy can open you more to everyday magic! You are a spiritual being having a physical experience. Reality is not the solid world you believe it to be. Magic and miracles are WAY possible!

3. **Know you're loved unconditionally by God.** You deserve it whether you believe it or not, so BELIEVE IT! Know that your worthy of all good things, so be open to them.

4. **Set goals.** Ask for what you want. Write out a wish list. Affirm your desires and intentions. Say them out loud or silently in your mind before sleep and or on waking. In whatever way you like, affirm what you want - to yourself and the universe. When you set goals and specify desired outcomes, and visualize these, the universe will start arranging things for your benefit. You co-create your reality by visualizing your dreams regularly, clearing limiting beliefs that stand in the way, and feeling the outcomes ahead of time to call them into existence in the present. My friend taught me to ASK FOR MORE! So I say, "this or something better ".

5. **Have FUN!** What brings you happiness and joy? Bring more of it into all areas of your life. You don't need money to have fun. Go to a park, meet someone for a cup of coffee. Your thoughts create your happiness so think positive, joyful thoughts.

6. **Start awakening to the messages you receive through symbols.** Become a detective of your outer reality! Learn to decipher hidden meanings and messages in the people and circumstances you attract.

Even the title of a book someone's reading next to you, email subject lines, overheard snippets of conversation, a song that comes on the radio, advertising headlines, a flyer that crosses your path etc., can all hold relevance. And remember to ASK for answers and to be shown signs and symbols. Whenever I have asked my dad to help me (he's been in Spirit since 2001) the way I know the answer is a song that I connect only to him will come on the radio and it's an OLD song. I love it when that happens!

Life is not just some random set of experiences separate from you. As quantum physics now proves, you and your world are linked! Understanding the communications in your world is not only fascinating and illuminating, but for me has been totally LIFE-CHANGING! I have had countless magical moments and synchronicities and opportunities by opening my eyes and mind to this guidance. When we listen to this guidance it will help guide you to what's for your highest good!

My company, The Spiritual Awakening, tagline is "Awaken to Your Higher Self and Spread Your Wings."

Some Things Intuitive People Do

They listen to that inner voice.

They take time for solitude.

They create.

They practice mindfulness.

They observe everything.

They listen to their bodies.

They connect deeply with others.

They pay attention to their dreams.

They enjoy plenty of down time.

They mindfully let go of negative emotions.

CHAPTER 2
PSYCHIC OR MEDIUM?

I am a psychic and a spiritual medium and first I'd like to explain the difference between the two because a lot of people think they are one in the same. An important difference is all mediums are psychic but not all psychics are mediums!

Everyone is psychic. Some people call it a gut feeling or mother's intuition, but we all have it to some degree. Some of us come by it naturally and through practice we develop it further. Practice does make perfect, even with psychic abilities. Some examples of psychic ability are:

• You have the feeling that the phone is going to ring...and it does.

• You think about a person and they call you right then.

• You start to hum a song in your head only to turn on the radio, and there it is...the same song.

• Perhaps you've started wondering out of the blue what happened to your old friend from high school, and then you bump into her at the mall the next day.

Are these coincidences? No! There are no coincidences. You are tuning in to your own intuition. Perhaps you have felt it in your solar plexus, the place right above your navel. I've used my intuition when deciding whether to go on the express lane of Route 80 or not. If I feel butterflies in my solar plexus, then I take the local lanes which always winds up being the faster route. When we listen to our intuition we cannot go wrong.

It's all about getting used to information coming to you from a different source. The more you practice, the easier it becomes. When the phone rings, pause a few seconds before answering. Can you tell who it is? Try it at work. Can you tell which elevator door will open first? Are you able to pick up on a person's mood without them saying anything? Did you ever notice people who are together for years tend to finish each other's sentences? They are reading each other psychically.

With that said, psychics do not read your mind. However, they may receive impressions about what is going on in your life for which you may need guidance. If you are going to get a psychic reading or have a session with a medium it's best to make a list of questions. Write down important information to reference. During a reading you may be emotional and have expectations that may cause you to suffer from psychic amnesia. Be open to who comes through. It doesn't always need to be a huge revelation. Spirit may relate a small thing that happened that day so you know they do see what is going on in your life. It could be something as silly as you were telling your husband and the kids they need to take their shoes off at the door because you discovered gum on the rug earlier that day! Your mother in Spirit sees how difficult it is for you to constantly clean up after the hubby and the kids and will mention it during a session. I always get a kick out of the fact that just because a parent is in Spirit does not mean they stop parenting!

A medium is able to connect to those in Spirit, those that have crossed over. They do this by raising their vibration and Spirit lowers their vibration in order to communicate. I personally choose prayer and meditation as a conduit. Sometimes I don't have a chance to pray beforehand. I could be in line at the supermarket and a Spirit will attempt to get my attention. Then I say a prayer and shield myself immediately. As with people who are here on earth there are good and bad, I believe that there are those in Spirit I don't want to have anything to do with. It is very important to have discernment. You wouldn't walk through an airport with your wallet wide open. It's the same with protecting yourself psychically. Of course your own guides will help you too. Make sure to develop a closer relationship with your guides. Just as you travel with people you know and trust, when you develop a relationship with your own guides they are your helpers. My guides are with me to help, they are people who are my relatives and loved ones.

Let me explain how I knew I had the ability to connect with Spirit and that I had a special guide. When I was nine years old my Grandma passed away. At that time we lived in an apartment. There was an outside door and inside door into the apartment. My brothers and sisters and I would always know it was Grandma because we would hear the rustling of shopping bags loaded down with goodies. I remember shortly after her death I clearly heard the outside door open and I ran to the inside door because I FELT my Grandma and heard the rustling of bags.

Even though Grandma wasn't physically there I felt her wonderful hug! Grandma gave the best hugs! As a child I didn't question this. I KNEW Grandma was around me watching out for us just like she always did. This brings me such comfort always. I still love Grandma's hugs. Thanks Grandma!

To begin practicing you'll want to be able to concentrate, be by yourself in a quiet room and push all thoughts away. Forget the laundry list of things you need to do. This is your time. Thoughts flow at an incredible rate. Each individual is sending and receiving thoughts from outside of his mind. We can all tap into this collective consciousness. Many people think you need to meditate on something for a long period of time before you get something; actually it is the exact opposite. Don't try to focus on anything in particular. Trust that what you are receiving is correct! This comes with practice and validation. Also it is important to remember it's not about you! If you're giving a message it may sound stupid or crazy to say to the client, "I am getting brown and bubble gum." It may be that the person is getting new carpet because they can't get the bubble gum stain out of the brown carpet. TRUST what you get. It only has to make sense to the other person. Sometimes it may not make sense right away. If it doesn't, just say "I'll leave you with that then, please write it down." Don't worry - just ask them to call you to let you know if you were correct.

You could also do this: while you're out taking a walk notice and really look at what's going on around you. Take the time to notice everything. Really look at the people passing by you. What color are their clothes? Notice the color and the style of their hair. Can you smell coffee, someone's perfume? What sounds do you hear around you? The hum of an air conditioner, the birds chirping? People laughing? Can you sense the weather? Is the air moist? Once you take the time to notice the physical energies around you, you'll find it easier to tap in psychically and to Spirit.

Have you ever thought you saw a flash of light or color out of the corner of your eye, knowing there wasn't anyone around to cause that? Well perhaps you just saw a Spirit pass by. They move very quickly, remember I said their energy vibration is extremely fast. As you practice noticing everything around you with ALL six senses you'll be able to tune into your own psychic ability and Spirit better. Remember to take stock of how you are feeling. Are you more energized when you go out for lunch? Could it be the energies of your environment are affecting you? Recognize how you feel physically at certain times and certain places. When you become aware of the changes of the energy around you, you may begin to notice when Spirit comes close to you. You may feel a tingling sensation, the hairs on your body may stand up. You may feel warmer or colder. These are just some examples of how your clairsentience is kicking in. You may be mostly clairaudient, you may hear words or names or sounds when Spirit is near. By the way, always thank those helpers. Gratitude is important to all of us, here and there!

So you may be wondering how you know it is a Spirit and not just your imagination. The answer is that you'll have a knowing feeling come over you. I sometimes have a sensation in my ear as if Angel wings are fluttering rapidly. Sometimes I hear them speaking as clearly as I hear you talking to me or I'll see full apparitions appear. Sometimes I see and hear a word over a client's head and then I ask Spirit to please show me or tell me more. I have been known to communicate with Spirit in their native tongue which I do not speak. I ask them to say it or spell the word phonetically to me. This is always very interesting to me as well. I once was doing a reading for five sisters when I started to speak Arabic. I didn't know I spoke Arabic! I have spoken German and Italian as well. Very often I use the exact mannerisms of the person in

Spirit. These are just more validations for the person getting the reading. So be OPEN to things out of the ordinary happening as you develop your own abilities!

CHAPTER 3
HOW PSYCHIC MESSAGES ARE RECEIVED

I will be using the words psychic, intuitive and empathic interchangeably. Intuitive information is always present within your mind, you just may not be aware of it. I am going to be talking about the unconscious and conscious mind.

It is no coincidence that I chose as my other career to become an Advanced Clinical Hypnotherapist.

The challenge in using your psychic senses is that intuitive information is mostly received and stored in your unconscious. The way to tap into that information is by listening to a very subtle dialog that is occurring in your head. It is possible that you have many voices or thoughts going on in your mind at all times, drowning out the intuitive information available to you. I like to call this all the crappy minutiae. That internal conversation is the result of your conscious and unconscious communicating with each other in a continuous loop. You may or may not have noticed this dialog before. Most of us notice the nagging, critical version of our thoughts and feelings. You know those self-defeating thoughts; most of us are preoccupied with that voice. Yet there is a more powerful REAL voice just underneath all that inner mental chatter. It is a very small soft "voice" referred to as the small, still voice within. It is your intuition. It can be an urge to pick up the phone and call someone and when you do they tell you they were just thinking about you. Or perhaps you are "told" by your intuition to avoid a certain place at a certain time. Often we ignore that voice and think later that we should have listened. It's more of a feeling than a sound, yet I would describe it as something somewhere in-between. One of the many day-to-day ways I use my intuition is by asking if I should take a certain route to somewhere. I know we have GPS but this is my own GPS.

How often have you said something like, "I kept thinking that I should call you but I just didn't," or, "something kept telling me to drive down that street but I just thought I was being silly?" This tiny little messenger comes from the conversation loop between your conscious and unconscious mind. It is difficult to listen to this voice because it speaks a different language. An important distinction between the "conscious mind voice" and the" unconscious mind voice" is as follows:

The "conscious mind voice," the rational waking mind, speaks loud and clear. Its primary job is to analyze things and then see how to take action.

The "unconscious mind voice," the intuitive subconscious mind, speaks in whispers and metaphors. Its primary job is to reveal things to you.

When the intuitive voice is trying to tell you something it is often a matter of guessing the message. It is very much like talking to someone who speaks a different language than you. Occasionally you can get the gist of what they are trying to say but it is mostly guess work. This is where most of us struggle with intuition. We are often aware that we are receiving or sensing some information but do not know how to interpret it. Your intuition whispers to you when you are awake. It is your guide.

So PAY ATTENTION!

When you sleep you travel into your unconscious where the barrier between you and your intuition disappears. In your sleep you experience your unconscious through dreams. Once you awaken that language fades into the background and becomes the dream voice again.

Sometimes you catch little glimpses of information, get hunches or feelings about things.

For those of us who have searched for the psychic side of ourselves, the journey has often been lonely and long. When you are awake you are using your conscious mind. Your unconscious mind is not usually visible during this time. When you sleep the waking mind takes a back seat and the unconscious mind emerges. This is also what happens in hypnosis! During sleep and dreams you wander in psychic territory. This is why dreams have a lot of psychic information. When you wake up again, the unconscious recedes and so does the psychic part.

In your consciousness, your dream voice is the connector between your conscious and unconscious minds. In your normal waking state the unconscious is still present, but acts as a hidden force until you do something to access it. Occasionally it spills over or makes itself known to the conscious mind.

Psychic information is always present in your mind but you may have to do something to access it. Sometimes it will be spontaneous in a hunch, a feeling or a bit of information. The point of becoming a Psychic is to learn to retrieve the information at will.

Making Sense of your Psychic Ability

Psychic Ability is defined as Insight, ESP, clairvoyance, discernment, divination, feeling, foreknowledge, gut reaction, hunch, innate knowledge, inspiration, instinct, intuitiveness, perceptivity, premonition, second sight, or sixth sense.

We are all born with an inner sense of knowing. We all have experienced a gut feeling at one time or another; I should <u>not</u> have bought that car. Or you knew it was <u>not</u> a good idea to book that trip when only a few days later you could have saved hundreds of dollars. We use our psychic abilities every day we just call it by another name. A feeling, an instinct, a hunch are some ways to we tap into our psychic ability.

<u>Exercise 1: Identifying Your Strengths</u>

Different ways you receive information/senses may include:
- Clairsentience-touch;
- Clairaudience - hear sound-voices;
- Claircognizance- knowing\thoughts you get; and
- Clairvoyance-clear seeing-between eyebrows.

Practice putting your focus on your internal world and trust your intuition.

Things you can practice with...

How many emails will you get that day?

Guess who's calling before you answer?

Guess who you will see that day unexpectedly?

What song will come on the radio next?

Which elevator door will open first?

When you ask a question how does it feel? Does your solar plexus have a positive or negative sensation?

If someone says show me your psychic ability you may not be able to show them in that instance. Many things are "invisible" to the senses but that does not mean they are nonexistent. I always say that I cannot see electricity but when I turn on the switch the light comes on! I have always believed it is not my job to convince anyone of my psychic or Medium abilities. It is enough for me to know them. However, there are all kinds of things people believe about psychic phenomenon that are **not true**.

Here are some of the most popular _false_ beliefs:

Psychic ability is a gift that only some people have. Because it is a natural part of being human, everyone has psychic abilities. Some people are more likely to pay attention than others and therefore may develop their abilities more easily. Different personalities will react to psychic potentials in different ways. A person who is more feeling-oriented may pay more attention to psychic messages. A person who focuses in their intellect may ignore psychic messages unless they are very intense. This can be compared to listening to a whisper versus waiting to be hit with a brick. Personally, I have always preferred listening to the whisper than getting hit on the head with a brick!

Psychic ability means the ability to see into the future. While premonitions of future events do occur, this is the least common of psychic events. The majority occurs by obtaining information already happening.

Psychic ability is unlimited and unconditional. Many people seem to think that if someone is psychic, that this means they have unlimited powers that work unconditionally one hundred percent of the time.

I hate to be the one to tell you, but no human ability works that way. Vision and hearing have limits and conditions, and so does psychic ability. Psychic abilities are influenced by as many factors as influence any person. Examples of what conditions influence psychic ability are: how relaxed or tense a person is, what a person pays attention to, a person's belief systems, emotional states, values, needs, desires, perceptions, and so on.

Philosophical and religious beliefs may act as a barrier to psychic information. An example of such a belief would be the thought that psychic abilities come from an evil force. If a person believes that psychic phenomena come from an evil force then they'll resist psychic experiences or give into fear of what might happen if they "tune in" to their psychic abilities. I have had many clients tell me they had a psychic experience and it frightened them so they shut down anything else. Many people are superstitious. It is important to understand that being superstitious and pursuing psychic development are two separate activities. Misinformation is the result of incorrect examples and stereotypes. Movies and television sometime portray psychic events as dramatic, intense and frightening.

The truth is, most psychic events are very subtle and usually related to ordinary situations. The media frequently ties in psychic abilities with the media's version of "occult practices." As you learn to access your psychic abilities there will not be any special effects or earth shattering visions in most of your experiences.

Another obstacle to psychic evidence deals with **fear of the unknown**. This is an instinctive fear that we all have on some level. I tell people that it is good to have a healthy skepticism and to go to a psychic that has been recommended to you. I personally do not tell clients "bad" things, I always say a prayer that the messages I receive and deliver be for their highest good. My intention is to always have the client leave happier and feeling better than when they first walked through the door. I truly care about them and it is reflected in my approach during the session.

A person's set of religious beliefs may play a role in how they perceive psychic abilities. Over the years I have had a few people say to me that "talking to dead people" was against their religion and that's why they would not come to me to ask anything. They were taught that the devil was involved.

Well, my answer is that I am a Spiritual person. I talk to God and the Angels on a regular basis. And I always say a prayer before seeing a client and teaching a class. I know I am here to help and I thank God for all my many blessings and abilities every day.

Intuitively Improve Your Life

1. Trust your intuition

Listen to that voice inside you. Follow your heart, gut, instincts and intuition. This can help with both your business and personal life.

2. Pray

Pray for help and for what you want (for the highest good of all). Give your worries and cares to God and the Angels to sort out for you.

3. Meditate and Relax

Prayer is us talking to God. Sometimes God answers during our meditations, walks in nature, or while we are relaxing. Watch and listen for answers and ideas popping into your head and then act on them.

4. Count Your Blessings (again)

We know that an attitude of gratitude helps us to relax, feel good, and opens the door to receiving more. Count five things you can be grateful for today. For example: eyes that are able to see, arms able to feel, the love others have for you. Sometimes I say I'm grateful the day is over and God willing I'll have another opportunity tomorrow

5. Help Others

Do something today to help another. Think of those less fortunate than yourself, and do something to help.

6. Focus on what is important

Focus on what really matters – health, family, happiness, friendships, serving clients to the best of your abilities. Focus on treating people well. And remember to SMILE! It's good for you and everyone you meet! My motto is, "If you see someone without a smile, give them one of yours!"

7. Gaining more business and new clients.

Think of what you offer, and how you can help people. Imagine the sorts of people you want to help. Imagine a beam of divine light shining down on you. Then imagine beaming these thoughts about how you can help people out into the world. Wait until you feel a click or connection has been made with someone. Then wait for them to get in touch.

8. Breathe – Relax – have a one minute holiday

When we get busy or stressed, we breathe more shallowly, get tense, and make poorer decisions. Take a minute to take some deep breaths ...relax....recall a favorite holiday or pleasant memory for 30 seconds.

9. What would God do?

When faced with a situation or difficult decision, ask yourself what would God or an Angel do, this may help you to come up with a better answer.

10. Ask the Angels for help, and watch for guidance, signs and miracles. And always remember to say "thank you!"

How to flex your INTUITIVE muscle:

Each day for an entire week notice the times you get a feeling or an intuitive impression about something. Then notice what shows up. This is not about accuracy. It's about discernment. When you notice how often your intuition works, you will begin to feel more comfortable with your impressions.

Be AWARE! Practice, practice, practice!

CHAPTER 4
PSYCHIC TOOLS

Since you were drawn to this book, you want to expand your psychic abilities but may not be sure where to start. With so many psychics being featured in many television shows and movies it can be quite overwhelming to pick which tool to use. Tarot, astrology, numerology and runes are all fascinating tools to work with, but they require a lot of time to learn and a lot of practice to be proficient in. Fortunately, not all psychic tools require hours of study but all of them do require practice. The methods below are great for beginners, and most gifted psychics have been using these tools in their daily practices for years.

Meditation

Whether you're new at developing your psychic abilities or you've been doing it for years, meditation is an important part of every psychic's daily practice. Prayer for me is another name for meditation. I always "tap in" to Divine Love daily and again before each Intuitive session with a client or to gain clarity for myself.

-        **What it is:** Meditation is a form of clearing your mind so that you can connect directly to source and receive messages from angels, spirits, God and other beings. It also helps to open your third eye chakra (between your eyebrows) and your Crown Chakra (located at the top of your head) which are associated with gaining insight and messages from beyond.

-       **How it works:** There are many different forms of meditation but if you're new to the practice, guided meditations may be the best choice for you. There are many CD's on the market you can download and practice with. This can be extremely challenging at first as your mind will have a natural tendency to become distracted. I call this the "laundry list." If you find your mind wandering focus on your breathing. Go at your own pace, taking your time and start small. It is NOT necessary to meditate for hours, a few minutes of concentrated quieting of your mind, and you will begin to decipher messages from God or your Higher Self or the Angels and Spiritual Guides.

Oracle Cards

If you've ever wanted to dabble with tarot, then you may want to start with oracle cards first. Doreen Virtue has many oracle card decks that are easy to work with. So you may want to check out her collection on Amazon or at your local metaphysical or book store such as Barnes and Noble. Personally I have a large collection which I use for my personal questions instead of using my own deck I designed and developed (with the help of my Spiritual guides) and had professionally made to use in my practice. My cards are shown on the cover of this book.

-     **What they are:** Oracle cards usually come in decks of 30-50 cards. Unlike tarot cards, they are not divided into any suits and most oracle decks focus on positive meanings and outcomes. Each card has a picture and a word or sentence to tell you what it means. They are useful in gaining insight to your situations.

-     **How They Work:** Think of your question as you shuffle your oracle cards. Once you get that intuitive thought that tells you that you've shuffled enough (you may feel a gentle vibe in your gut that signals you to stop, or you may actually hear a voice say "stop") you can draw one or more cards from the top of the deck, or split the deck and draw your cards there.

Personally, I like to use three oracle cards when asking a question. The first card represents a lesson that you learned in the past. The second card represents suggested action from your angels, guides or Higher Self. The third card represents the probable outcome.

Although each card typically has a word or sentence that tells you what it means, you can also take a look at the picture and see if the picture is telling you something. I have done many oracle readings in which I got more information from the picture than I did from the words or statements printed on the cards. Most oracle card decks include a manual to look up further meanings of each card. When I teach my psychic development classes, I tell my students not to look in the book until they feel they have received all the information from holding and looking at the pictures on the card.

Crystals

Crystals have been used for healing since the beginning of time. Each variety of crystal has a unique internal structure, which causes it to resonate at a certain frequency. It is this resonance that gives crystals their healing abilities. Applying this resonance in a certain way can help to restore and balance the body's energy systems (known as chakras). Crystals can be placed on specific points of the body to bring relief or can be carried in a pocket or worn as jewelry to help with a physical condition. Specific color crystals can be used for chakra healing. They can be placed on the body when you lie down on specific chakras. You may also use a combination of crystals. To begin hold a crystal gently in your hands (placing one hand under the other hand) as you meditate to give your Chakras a gentle stimulation to balance them.

Crystals by Color

Red and Black Crystals stimulate your root chakra to improve fertility, sex drive and ease menstral problems and increase courage. Ideal crystals include: garnet, ruby, red jasper, obsidian and hematite.

Orange Crystals stimulate the sacral chakra which helps to increase energy, dispels inhibitions and eases kidney trouble. Ideal crystals include: carnelian, tiger's eye, yellow jasper and citrine.

Yellow Crystals stimulate your stomach and your solar plexus chakra. This helps with digestive system problems and muscle cramps. Ideal crystals include: light citrine, light amber and agate.

Green and Pink Crystals stimulate the heart chakra and balance heart and emotional problems. They also help with chest conditions. Ideal crystals include: jade, aventurine, rose quartz, malachite and watermelon tourmaline.

Blue Crystals stimulate the throat chakra to ease ear, nose, throat and glandular conditions. Ideal crystals include: sodalite, azurite and lapis lazuli.

<u>Violet-Purple Crystals</u> stimulate the third eye chakra to improve concentration and mental awareness. They also ease pain, agitation and stress. Ideal crystals include: amethyst, florite, sugilite and labradorite.

<u>White Crystals</u> stimulate the crown chakra to increase a general sense of well-being. They also help with self-esteem and communication and to eliminate mental anguish or depression. Ideal crystals include: quartz, zircon and diamond.

Headaches

The crystal used to provide relief from a headache depends on the cause of the headache. A tension headache can be relieved by placing amethyst, amber or turquoise on or around the head. Lapis lazuli has been used for centuries to help treat migraines. Amethyst can be placed in a healing layout on and around the head to help relieve symptoms.

Another common cause of headaches is an imbalance between head energy and the solar plexus chakra usually brought about by stress or unsuitable food. If you suspect stress to be the cause of your headache or if you have a headache with an upset stomach use a stone that helps to balance the solar plexus such as citrine or moonstone.

Difficulty sleeping

Again, the crystal needed depends on the cause of the sleeplessness. You may need to experiment, as a stone that works well for one person may not work for someone else. If you believe tension and worry are stopping you from sleeping, place a crystal such a rose quartz, citrine or amethyst by the bed or under the pillow to calm and sooth.

If you believe your restlessness is a result of overeating, iron pyrite or moonstone can be used to calm the stomach.

If nightmares are causing you problems, protective crystals such as tourmaline or smoky quartz can promote peaceful sleep and should be placed at the foot of the bed. Labradorite may also help, as it is thought to chase away any unwelcome feelings and thoughts.

Lack of energy

Red, orange and yellow crystals can be used to promote an increase in energy. The most stimulating and dynamic crystals are those with bright, strong colors such as deep red garnet, golden amber or golden-yellow topaz.

For an increase in practical motivation use deeper tones like tiger's eye, dark citrine and jasper. Holding a clear quartz crystal, point upwards, in each hand and placing a citrine on the solar plexus can achieve a quick boost of energy to the whole system.

Concentration

Concentration can be aided by quartz, which is believed to give mental clarity, and carnelian, which clears extraneous thought.

Citrine and amber are thought to stimulate memory and lapis lazuli is a powerful amplifier of thoughts. Amethyst can promote mental clarity, helping you to focus on realistic goals and to visualize clearly. It is also believed to sooth the nervous system and to aid neural transmission.

Fluorite is an excellent aid to study, as it is believed to balance the functioning of the brain hemispheres while deep blue crystals such as sodalite can aid communication and give a better understanding of concepts and ideas.

Healing the mind

Crystals are believed to promote peace and tranquility by dissolving blockages to emotional expression. The crystals should be worn or kept about your person. They can also be placed in a healing layout.

Green is a healing color and many green crystals can be used to help reduce mental and nervous stress. In the East, green jade is prized for its ability to calm the nervous system and to focus the mind.

Rose quartz and blue lace agate can both be used for cleansing and detoxifying the emotions. Opal promotes emotional balance and stability and amethyst works on hormone production, balancing emotional highs and lows and helping you to feel less scattered and more in control. Amethyst can also relieve stress by reducing mental burdens and helping you to focus on realistic goals. Amber can be used to neutralize a negative state of mind and to balance any underlying emotional and endocrine imbalance.

To use for Desires and Situations

Abundance Jade or Citrine or Cinnabar

Addictions Aventurine

Allergies Chrysocolla

Astral Travel Angelite, Apophyllite, Green Calcite

Blood Pressure Dioptase, Turquoise

Peace and Calm Blue Lace Agate, Clear Quartz, Rose Quartz

Clairvoyance Amethyst, Azurite, Clear Quartz

Past Lives Amethyst, Obsidian

Weight control Labradorite

For more information on crystals check your local libraries or book stores. One of my favorite books is *Crystal Therapy* by Doreen Virtue and Judith Lukomski. Some other great books are; *The Crystal Bible* by Judy Hall and *The Pocket Book of Crystals* by Robert Simmons.

To get children interested in crystals there are several great books I've bought for my own grandchildren. I recommend *National Geographic Kids Everything Rocks and Minerals* by Steve Tomecek and *National Geographic Readers: Rocks and Minerals* by Kathleen Weidner Zoehfeld.

Cleansing your Crystals

Crystals should be treated with care. Many are fragile and/or water-soluble and some, such as amethyst, can fade in direct sunlight. When not in use it is a good idea to wrap your crystals in silk or velvet to protect them and to stop them from absorbing foreign vibrations.

When you receive your crystal it will have been around for many years. It may have been handled by many different people and might have absorbed some of their negative vibrations. It is important, therefore, to spend a little time cleansing your crystal. Cleansing can and should be done on a regular basis. If your crystal is looking dull it may be because it has picked up and absorbed negative energy from the surrounding environment. Try not to let anyone touch your crystal, even though they may be full of good intentions. If your crystal has been handled by someone else then cleanse it to clear any absorbed negative energy. There are several ways to do this:

• Bury your crystal in the ground. Putting your crystal in the ground overnight clears your crystal of any negative energy. Remember to mark the spot well.

• Hold your crystal under running water: most crystals can be held under running water, preferably naturally running water, but if this is not possible a running tap will do. Imagine a waterfall falling over your crystal until you feel that all the negative energies have been washed away. Please make sure that your crystal is not water-soluble before cleansing in this way. A clue to the water solubility of a crystal can be found in its name. Most water-soluble crystals end in "ite", such as fluorite, calcite, angelite and sodalite, selenite, kunzite, and apophyllite. Lapis lazuli is also water-soluble.

• Place in brown rice or sea salt: if you crystal is crumbly, layered or water soluble place in a bowl of brown rice or sea salt in order to cleanse it.

• Use crystals that cleanse other crystals: some crystals such as clear quartz or carnelian have the ability to cleanse other crystals. You can place a small crystal on top of a quartz cluster and leave it overnight or keep a carnelian in a bag of other crystals. This is an extremely useful method for delicate crystals but the cleansing crystals may need cleansing themselves afterwards.

- Sound: the vibrations of a pure sound can be used to cleanse a stone. You can use a bell, gong or tuning fork. Crystals can also be cleansed using the pure sound and vibration of Tibetan cymbals. Holding the cymbals over a group of crystals and bringing them together to make a sound, makes it possible to cleanse several crystals at once.

- Moonlight: both moonlight and sunlight can be used to cleanse your crystals. However, sunlight can fade some crystals, whereas moonlight is a powerful safe cleanser. The best time for using the moon to cleanse your crystals is the evening before a full moon, the evening of the full moon and the evening following a full moon because the energy is the most powerful at this time.

After you have cleansed your crystals, leave them for an hour or two in the sun to re-energize.

Two of my favorite crystals are Labradorite and carnelian. **Labradorite** aids in the power of spiritual vision. Labradorite opens spiritual pathways and attunes you to your Soul's purpose in incarnating.

It connects you with the greater part of your Soul so you can receive guidance from your Higher Self. Labradorite activates the Third Eye and allows you to access the highest levels of consciousness. It facilitates metaphysical working of all kinds. If you are inappropriately dependent on someone or something, Labradorite helps you detach and stand in your own power. Labradorite protects the Soul, no matter where it journeys. It also detaches thought forms from the aura. It is particularly useful if you are moving through challenging life conditions, as it connects you to your Highest Self's guidance and support.

Place labradorite on the Third Eye to assist eye issues and migraines that arise from blocked psychic power. Labradorite assists in regulating metabolism, hormonal balance and relieves symptoms of PMS. It helps to reduce inflammation and protects against colds.

Carnelian is used for motivation and clarification for goals. A glassy, translucent stone, carnelian is an orange-colored variety of chalcedony, a mineral of the quartz family. Its color varies from pale pinkish-orange to a deep rusty brown, though it is most known for its brilliant orange and red-orange crystals.

Carnelian crystals are stones of action that will give you the courage and confidence to move forward on a new path in life. In ancient times it was a stone used to protect the dead on their journey to the after-life. Carnelian's main qualities are energizing and grounding/centering. Carnelian also has protective qualities, and can fill one with warmth, joyful gratitude and a genuine simple happiness. It is a stone that activates one's flow of inner power and sexual power and is often recommended for women.

It is strong stone to aid the physical body, as it maintains an improved flow of life force energy via the blood. The vibration of this bright orange stone, will accelerate your motivation, and aid you to clarify your goals so you can find your best direction in life. It will aid you to make new, clearer decisions and better future career choices.

Feng shui-wise, carnelian is used for its energy activating and protective qualities. It is often used along with citrine for wealth and the flow of abundance.

Pendulums

A pendulum is a simple tool that can be used for receiving "yes," "no" and "maybe" responses from your Higher Self. It is a string or chain weighted by a heavy object called a bob. The bob may be a crystal or some form of gold, silver, brass, or other metal. I have several different ones that I use for my personal use as well as my business. My favorite pendulum is shown on the cover photo of this book. The following steps illustrate how to use a pendulum.

1. Choose A Pendulum:

Go with what you desire and are attracted to. If you like the way a pendulum looks or feels to you, and you are instinctively drawn to it, then that is the one for you.

2. Cleanse Your Pendulum:

You may cleanse it by holding it under running cold water from a tap, soaking it in sea salt water or burying it directly in sea salt. I personally use visualization and intent. As you hold your pendulum just imagine pure cleansing energies of love and light coming from your heart down your arms and through your pendulum to cleanse it. Affirming your intention for its Divine pure guidance simultaneously.

3. Understand the Directional Swings of Your Pendulum:

Pendulums primarily swing in vertical straight lines, horizontal straight lines, and in circular movements (clockwise or counter-clockwise).

4. Clarify the Directional Swings of Your Pendulum:

Check which direction of your pendulum's swing indicates a yes or no. You can do this by asking the pendulum and your Higher Self to show you. Hold the pendulum chain or string between your thumb and forefinger around 5 or 6 inches above the actual pendulum object.

Think or say "please show me a yes," and, holding that mental intention, observe what direction your pendulum begins to swing in. Stay with this until you get a clear response. It may take a little while so practice being patient. When the pendulum moves, write down which direction it went. Was it in a straight line or was it in a circular motion? Then pause and hold the pendulum still. I ask the pendulum to stop but you may bring it to a stop manually.

Repeat this procedure now, with the thought (and if you wish, words) of "please show me a no," to ascertain the direction for a no response. Then continue for a neutral response. Ask "please show me a neutral response," for example. You may wish to prop your elbow on the table to have a steady hold.

You can continue to test yes and no responses by asking questions you know the answers to, such as "is my name [your name]." This should give you a yes response. Saying the wrong name should give you a no response.

Pendulum Response Examples:
Clockwise circular movement signifies yes. Counter-clockwise circular movement signifies no. If it remains still it signifies neutral.
Or
Clockwise circular movement signifies no. Counter-clockwise circular movement signifies yes.
Vertical/horizontal swing signifies neutral.
Or
Vertical swing signifies yes. Horizontal swing signifies no. If it remains still it is neutral.

This is how my personal pendulum swings. Another way of looking at a neutral response is: it has yet to be determined.

5. Alignment

For the most reliable answers, you want to be in a balanced and centered space, and not one that is emotionally charged, particularly in relation to the questions you will be asking. You might want to meditate first or breathe deeply to calm, relax and still the mind. To affirm the truth of this process you may say, "may these questions be answered in the name of love, light and all that is good and true, for the highest good of all."

I also recommend you clearly intend and affirm that the communication you receive via your pendulum be from your Higher Self by saying the White Light Prayer. You can connect to your Higher Self by intention, as well as by addressing your Higher Self directly with each question. You may start each question by saying, "Dear Higher Self...", or by affirming your intention beforehand by saying "I affirm that all responses received via this pendulum be from my Higher Self." Use words that feel right and true to you.

These steps can safe-guard against ego interference and other entities.

6. Prepare Your Questions:

A question should be one that can be answered with a positive, negative or neutral response. As a quick note, avoid 'shoulds' and 'coulds' in your questioning (i.e. "should I go on holiday to Alaska this August?"). Instead use variations like those provided below:

"Is it for my highest good to go on holiday to Alaska this August?"

"Is it beneficial for me to go on holiday to Alaska this August?

"Is going on holiday to Alaska this August aligned to my highest path?"

"Is going on holiday to Alaska this August an optimum choice for me at this time?"

"Is going on holiday to Alaska this August a positive option for me at this time?"

7. Ask Your Questions:

Be prepared to ask several questions in order to receive enough information. You may need to ask a few questions about the same subject to get accurate information. For example, and in the case of a dietary enquiry:

a) Is this cereal beneficial for my body? Response: no
b) Is the oat flour in the cereal beneficial for my body? Response: yes (oats are ok)
c) Is the barley in the cereal beneficial for my body? Response: yes (barley is ok)
d) Are the wheat flakes in the cereal beneficial for my body? Response: no (there is your answer. Your body cannot tolerate wheat products at this time; you may be allergic to wheat and can go on to test for that.)

Remember, however, that your body can tolerate some foods one day and not the next. Therefore, it may be important to use your pendulum daily if exploring dietary aspects, or to ask in your initial questions if you have general or an overall allergy to a given ingredient. I've been known to whip out my pendulum in the grocery aisle to see if it is a good choice for me at that time.

8. Between Questions:
Make sure to completely stop any pendulum swinging motion between each of your questions to clear any lingering energies that pertain to the previous question.

9. Relax and keep an open mind!

Aim to allow the process rather than 'try' or force it in any way. If you start feeling frustrated or stressed, you will jeopardize the clarity of responses; so just stop, relax and begin again. It does not require effort, but focus, clarity, willingness and openness. You are essentially 'receiving' insight. Beware of holding any strong expectations or being too emotionally invested with respect to answers as this could influence the clarity of responses or lead to frustration and disappointment if they are not as you wish. Ensure you are in a relaxed and neutral state of mind. Remember to ask a number of questions in any one area to gain more information and a bigger picture of the situation.

Determining Which Tool Is Right For You

We all receive psychic information in different ways. You may find that you like one method over another, or that all of them work equally as well. The secret is to practice and play with all of them so that you can get a feel of which tools, and methods are right for you. When it comes to readings, and receiving information intuitively, there really is no right or wrong way to do things. Whatever works for you is what is right for you. While some experts in the field may give you information to work with or to increase your knowledge of these tools, no one can tell you what method will work best for you. So play with them, have fun, and continue to explore. Practice! Practice! Practice!

CHAPTER 5
ALL ABOUT ANGELS

We each have Guardian Angels, who are here to protect us. If you've ever thought, "Phew that was a near miss or lucky escape!" then that was probably your Guardian Angel protecting you. We also have other, guiding Angels who are sent to help us. Any of these can talk with us and help guide our lives for the better. Frequently, the Archangels play a big part in working with us too. They are all here to help us. People also often have spirit guides, animal guides, and human guides to help them too. There is an abundance of help we can call on. I always start any communication with the White Light Prayer, which is as follows: I surround myself with the White Light of Truth, nothing but that which is of the truth and for my highest good shall approach me, for I am a child of God and God will protect me. Amen. (I know I told you this prayer in an earlier chapter, but trust me it bears repeating. It is that important!)

People ask me "what's the difference between guides and Angels?" Angels are beings who have never incarnated upon the earth. They can communicate with us and perform miracles that help us. The Archangels are powerful beings who are higher up in the Angel hierarchy. Spirit Guides are the souls of wise people who have lived many lives upon the earth before, and offer to help us with guidance and advice during this lifetime. They will often take forms such as Red Indians, wise men, or animal guides. They generally don't have the same miraculous powers as the Angels or Archangels.

What names do Angels have? Angels can have classic names, like Michael, Raphael or Serenity. They can also have human names, such as Angelica, Thomas or David. Often they have unusual sounding names, such as Arcadia or Azura. Azura is my personal Angelic guide whom I named my Angel cards after (they are on cover photo) .

What do the Angels look like? Can you see them? It's rare to see Angels in physical form. Mostly we see Angels in our mind's eye. Like humans, Angels vary in their appearance. Some are male, some female, some androgynous. Mostly they have wings, but sometimes not. Often they have flowing robes and a spiritual light and glow around them. Do Angels take on human form? Later I will share a story with you about just such an encounter I had.

So what is it like, communicating with Angels? Each Angel has a different feel or quality or sound – or color that's how you can tell them apart. Generally, people get the sort of Angel that is appropriate for THEM.

I believe that we are given a Guardian Angel at birth. People always ask me if our Guardian Angel ever leaves us? I believe our Guardian Angel is always with us throughout our lives. We have available to us a whole host of Angels whom we may call upon.

Sometimes, people also have deceased relatives who come back to support, help and guide them. My Grandma –who acted as an Angel while she was here on earth is not one. She is, however, one of my helpers and gatekeepers when I do any spiritual medium work. So how do we communicate with the Angels and Spirit Guides?

Everyone has guardian Angels, but many people are just too busy to hear them. Angels do not interfere in our daily lives, except in dire circumstances. They will, however, drop subtle messages to keep us out of trouble if we are alert enough to catch them.

If you want a clear and concise message from your Angel, you must ask a direct question. Your Angel will always answer your questions. Ask your question out loud if possible, as clearly and concisely as possible. Answers will always be tangible and explicit, something you can put your hands on. The answers I've gotten I could pick up and examine. Asking a frivolous question will get you a silly answer. The universe will match your level of sincerity. So be sincere.

Many people would like to believe in guardian Angels, but are skeptical. There are con artists on the astral plane, just as there are here. Your Angel will be happy to provide you with evidence of their existence. A real Angel will expect you to ask for proof, and will provide you with straightforward answers. Again say the White Light Prayer before attempting to communicate with them (White Light Prayer: *I surround myself with the White Light of Truth. Nothing but that which is of the truth and for my highest good shall approach me, for I am a child of God and God will protect me. Amen.*).

Here's the evidence of my own guardian Angel:

My children were all in school and it was a very hot day. With three growing boys we were constantly running out of milk. So on this day I decided to take a quick ride to town which is only five miles away, to pick up another gallon. I was on my way home when my car door locks frantically started to go up and down. This had never happened before so I pulled over to see if by turning off the ignition they would stop. I did this and as soon as I turned the key they did it again, up and down, up and down up and down furiously even more than before. So I pulled over once more, stopped the car, took the key out and just *before* I put it back in they started to go up and down again. Ok so this got my attention! There is no current of electricity to make them go up and down with the key out and in my hand! This is when I asked Spirit, what do you want me to do? The door locks stopped clicking up and down and I heard in my mind "stay put". So I did. My rational mind could have told me just get home and let my husband look at the car later. I didn't want the milk to spoil in this heat. But my intuition told me to listen to the voice in my head. A few minutes passed and I asked if it was ok to go. I sensed it was ok, so I put the key back in the ignition and started the car. The locks did not go up and down again the rest of the way home. In fact they had never done that before that day nor in the 10+ years that I owned the car. When I arrived home there was a huge tree branch that had fallen across my walkway in the few minutes I had been gone. Had the door locks not distracted me and kept me from coming home earlier, I would surely have been there when it happened. I knew immediately my Angels had saved me and I thanked them for protecting me once more. So the motto of this story is, pay attention to the signs and symbols your Angels send you, it could be a matter of life or death!

If you want to talk to your Angel, you must be prepared to listen, and be alert for their side of the conversation. The universe will answer your sincere questions, but only if you are listening. Be aware of symbols around you. Ask your Angel an honest question and you'll get an honest answer. What kinds of questions can you ask? Anything you want!

Angels offer us help 24/7; the more receptive we are, the more help they can give us. Create your own invocations or prayers that specifically call for the help you need.

Angels work with everyone regardless of personal histories and beliefs. Angels are infinite and omnipresent – your request does not diminish them in any way, nor does it affect their ability to be with and help everyone else at the same time.

They exist beyond our idea of time and space and respond to everyone with unconditional love. Place every worry and fear as well as every good intention into the hands of your Angels. Let go and release all expectations of how your request will be answered (I didn't say it was going to be easy). Have patience, there is our timing and then there is Divine Timing. Every prayer is answered. If you fear that your prayer will not be answered, then ask for help in understanding and seeing your answered prayer more clearly. Trust that you will see the love in every answered prayer. Angelic help is infinite and unlimited—you cannot use it up or run out of it. You cannot ask for "too much". It's ok to Ask for help. Always say thank you!

Oh, and yes, it is ok to ask for little things. I often ask my parking Angel for the perfect space. My friends thought I was a little crazy at first but once they saw how easy it was, now they all ask their parking Angel. This really is awesome when it is either bad weather or when going Christmas shopping at the mall. I do however ask that it is for my highest good and that no one else needs it more than I do!

When you receive some major guidance, ask for confirmation and ask for the best time to act.

You can either check with your intuition (does it feel right?) and/or ask the Angels for signs and answers. Then you will know. Simply ask, believe, receive and say thank you!

Here are some simple questions you can ask:
Is now the right time to act on this?
- If yes, what should I do next?
- If No, when is the right time to act on this? Within the next three months? Within the next six months? Next year?
If this is right, please give me some signs and confirmation.

Just by taking these two simple steps, you can learn to act on the guidance you are receiving at the right time, rather than delaying too long. You will feel better sooner, and your life will flow more easily and happily if you are following guidance, rather than ignoring or delaying it. When you are not sure when and how to act, ask the Angels.

"Please help guide me to make these changes in the most Divine perfect way possible for the highest good of all. Thank you."

"I invite the Angels to help me now, with the next steps of my life. For this I am so grateful, and so it is. Amen."

Which Angel is Around You?

There are many different types of Angels which can come to us to help us:

Your Guardian Angel - This Angel is with you from birth, and is the Angel who keeps you safe and protects you -it may have saved you from accidents or harm numerous times. Our guardian Angel is often one of the Angels that communicates with us and guides us too. Or keeps us from getting home too soon by playing with car door locks! It is so comforting to know that we are being looked out for. Someone always has our back!

Guiding Angel - We may have one, two or more other guiding Angels, who are here to help guide us in our lives. Often they will have different roles, for example one may help with your personal life, and one may help you with your work. I have an Angel called George who is my business helper. Whenever I have a major business decision I call on his guidance. If you ask them, they will tell you what they are here to help you with. I find that as you grow they change with your needs. I have other

Angels and Spirit guides now that are helping me write my books. I am ever so grateful for all their help.

Archangels - Archangels are high ranking Angels within the celestial hierarchy. They can work with thousands of people simultaneously. Talk to Archangel Michael even though thousands may be calling on him too! Archangels also frequently work as our guiding Angels too.

Higher Beings - people often have visits from other Angels too. They may be a messenger Angel, with you only for today, to bring you a special message, or a healing Angel, or another Angel sent to help you rarely or occasionally. As the Angel who was in the elevator at the hospital with me.

Once you start communicating regularly with the Angels, you will soon discover which ones are with you permanently, and which ones are more occasional visitors. But remember ALWAYS THANK THEM!

Which reminds me of another time I had an Angel who used my car lights to direct me to find someone's home. I realized the car lights started blinking when I mentally asked questions. For instance, if I thought "should I call someone and ask them to come over?" they would blink on and off rapidly. Once I realized it was not a technical problem I wound up asking directions to a client's home. She lived in a development around a lake with winding trails and no street lights. It was so dark. I was so lost.

Of course I didn't have a cell phone, so I couldn't even call. I figured what the heck let's see if this works for directions. So I would say out loud "do I turn right?" If the lights blinked I knew to turn right. Sure enough, they got me right to her front door. This went on for a few months. I had a mechanic look at it and he couldn't find anything wrong and of course it never happened to him.

Exercise 1: Communicating with Your Angels and Guides

Your Angels and Spirit Guides communicate with you in a way that is unique to you. So how can you tell for yourself? Here's an exercise for you to do.

Step 1: Find a quiet place to be.
Step 2: Take three big deep breaths and tune into your heart center. Put your focus there.
Step 3: Call in your Angels and Guides (you can say, "Angels and Spirit Guides please be with me now").

Step 4: Ask your Angels to show you how they communicate with you (yes, you can simply say, "Angels please show me how you communicate with me"). You can also put your hand over your heart as you say this.

Remember to feel any sensations in your body and be aware of any chills, or warmth or pictures, or a color or even a knowing that comes to you as you ask this question. It will be different for everyone that does this exercise (I personally get a sensation in my ear where I can picture tiny Angels fluttering their wings and I lose my outside hearing ability for just a moment or two).

You may ask them what their name is. Write it down. Repeat these steps to find out all the different Angels and Spirit Guides you have. Know that as we learn and grow in our own Spiritual journey we have different guides to help us. Most important of all, BE OPEN! No tingle is too small, no idea is too big. Guidance from the Angels and Spirit Guides will always be loving. Ask, Believe, Receive and always say Thank You!

Archangels

The Archangels are known by name to many of us. Following is a description of each of the Archangels, so that you may get familiar with them.

ARCHANGEL RAPHAEL

(Healing power of God; The Divine has healed) Hebrew word *rapha* means "doctor" or "healer". Raphael is a powerful healer and assists with all forms of healing - humans and animals. He helps to rapidly heal body, mind and spirit if called upon. You may call upon Raphael on behalf of someone else, but he can't interfere with that person's free will. If they refuse spiritual treatment, it can't be forced. Raphael can be called upon to help healers such as doctors, therapist and surgeons. Call on Raphael if you're a student entering the healing field and you're looking for the right school and or are in need of help with studies, as well as getting the time and money for school. He also assists with establishing healing practices when your schooling is finished. Raphael not only helps you to heal from physical, emotional and mental pain, he also heals wounds from past lives. Part of Raphael's healing work involves spirit releasing and space clearing. He often works with Michael to exorcise discarnate entities and escort away lower energies from people and places. The chummiest and funniest of all Angels, Raphael is often pictured chatting merrily with mortal beings. He's very sweet, loving, kind, and gentle and you know that he's around when you see sparkles or flashes of green light. Raphael

is known as the "Patron of Travelers" as well as a healer. Call upon Raphael when you are traveling, to assure safe travel. In addition, he assures that all your transportation, lodging and luggage details go miraculously well. Raphael also helps with inward spiritual journeys, assisting in searches for truth and guidance. Other areas Raphael helps with is finding lost pets, reducing and eliminating addictions and cravings, clairvoyance, and bringing unity to your life. If you feel out of touch with your spirituality, if you've lost a partner and or your soul body doesn't feel "whole" call upon Archangel Raphael.

Once when my business partner and I were shopping for furniture for our office space, we saw an end table on display. Since we had previously put together furniture that took us hours to make, we really did not want to have to put another one together. This particular end table did not have any boxes below it so we hoped they would just sell us the display. The last one we had put together, the instructions made no sense and we were left with bolts and screws leftover. We looked at each other, said a quick prayer and asked for someone to come to that department to help us. Over the loud speaker we heard, "Raphael assistance is needed in the furniture department." We looked at each other and just knew he was going to help us. Indeed, he said normally they were not allowed to sell the display furniture but he was going to make an exception for us. We nearly kissed him we were so grateful! Remember, Ask, Believe, Receive and always say Thank You!

Archangel Raphael Healing Prayer

Archangel Raphael, I call upon you, I know that you are there, and ask you for your healing strength in answer to my prayer. Please take away the sadness, take away the pain, hold me in your healing wings and make me whole again For this I am so grateful and so it is. *Amen.*

ARCHANGEL URIEL
(God's light, Fire of God, The Angel of Peace)

Uriel is considered one of the wisest Archangels because of his intellectual information, practical solutions and creative insight, but he is very subtle. You may not even realize he has answered your prayer until you've suddenly come up with a brilliant new idea. An Aha moment! Uriel warned Noah of the impending flood and helped the prophet Ezra to interpret mystical predictions about the coming Messiah. He also brought the knowledge and practice of alchemy and the ability to manifest from thin air, as well as illuminates situations and gives prophetic information and warnings. All this considered, Uriel's area of expertise is divine magic, problem solving, spiritual understanding, studies, alchemy, weather, earth changes and writing. Considered to be the Archangel who helps with earthquakes, floods, fires, hurricanes and natural disasters, call on Uriel to avert such events or to heal and recover in their aftermath.

Archangel Uriel is the Archangel of peace, both on a planetary and a personal scale. He is also known by some as the 'psychologist Angel' as he can help to remove negative thoughts and beliefs, allowing us to experience greater inner peace. Call upon Uriel to help you release any negativity, and sooth your mind and your soul. He brings divine light into your life as he transforms painful memories and restores peace to your past. Whenever you feel you have lost your way, call on him and the Ruby Ray; invite his essence into your life to assist you in becoming a master of your energies.

Uriel appears as a large (shimmering) being of light, with less distinct features, surrounded by gold or yellow light which is Archangel Uriel's usual color. You can ask Uriel to work on you while you sleep, during meditation, or to lead you to what you need to help you.

Archangel Uriel Prayer

I call upon Archangel Uriel to assist me in anchoring myself in peace and love that is strong enough to withstand any negativity. I invoke this powerful light being to help me turn my worst disappointments into my greatest blessings and assist me in releasing blocks to forgiveness. For this I am so grateful and so it is. Amen.

ARCHANGEL ARIEL
(Lioness of God)

As the "Lioness of God," Archangel Ariel is often linked with boosting courage and confidence. If you enlisted Ariel's support, be observant of images of lions as a sign that she is with you. Because her aura is pale pink, Rose Quartz crystal is used to connect with her energy.

Archangel Ariel is the Angel of Environmentalism and Abundance and the patron Angel of wild animals. Furthermore, she is associated with instant manifestation through divine magic. You can ask Ariel to increase prosperity for yourself or loved ones.

Ariel is also believed to work with Archangel Raphael in the healing arts. Ariel is the feminine aspect of Uriel. Archangel Ariel is sometimes referred to as the tallest Angel so she can see all of creation. She is often shown wearing a white robe holding the Earth.

Ariel helps us understand the relationship between all forms of life and the different levels of spirits and realities that surround us. She shows us that our actions influence all life from the large trees to the smallest bacteria. Ariel will help you create peace in the world by starting within your own heart.

Try stones of: lapis lazuli, healing of self and planet for joy and courage; jade, for Earth wisdom and energy; and pearl, to help provide understanding and reverence of life. Any color of earth tones or pure white are connected with Archangel Ariel. House plants are a great way to connect with Earth.

Archangel Ariel Prayer

I call upon Archangel Ariel to give me courage to pursue my goals for my highest good. May abundance of all things good be in my life. Empower me to be a healing force for the Earth. For this I am so grateful and so it is. Amen.

ARCHANGEL GABRIEL
(Man of God; God Has Shown Himself)

Archangel Gabriel is one of the two highest ranking Angels. He is the leading Angel who stands in the presence of the God/Goddess as a co-coordinator. He is the Archangel of annunciation, humanity, resurrection, heavenly mercy, vengeance, death, revelation, truth, and hope. Bringer of news and heralds the revealing of answers. Maker of changes.

He is the Patron Saint of Communications. As a published author, I call upon Archangel Gabriel to help me with my writing.

Gabriel was the messenger angel who announced to Mary that she would bear a Son who would be conceived of the Holy Spirit, Son of the Most High, and the Saviour of the world. It was Gabriel who dictated the Koran to Muhammad. According to legend, it is Gabriel who will blow the horn announcing the second coming of Christ. His symbols are the lily and the trumpet.

Gabriel has been accredited as the Angel who selects souls from heaven to be birthed into the material world and spends the nine months as the child is being developed informing the new person of what he or she will need to know on Earth, only to silence the child before birth by pressing his finger onto the child's lips, thus producing the cleft below a person's nose.

If an idea about how to solve a problem comes to your mind, especially after you've been praying for guidance about solving a difficult problem, it may be a sign that Gabriel is with you. Gabriel often visits people while they're dreaming. He is considered the Archangel of dreams, premonitions, and clairvoyance.

He will help you grow in knowledge and wisdom. Your spiritual growth and development will progress faster than ever before when you call upon him. You may see either white or copper light around you when Gabriel is nearby since Gabriel's electromagnetic energy corresponds to the white Angel light ray and his aura is a copper color.

Archangel Gabriel Prayer

Archangel Gabriel I call upon you to surround me with a beautiful white light to clarify my Divine Purpose and dissolve any confusion, stress or worries that are affecting me. Give me the wisdom I need to make good decisions and the confidence I need to act on those decisions. Teach me how to communicate effectively when I have something important to say and to listen when others have something important to say to me. For this I am so grateful and so it is. Amen.

ARCHANGEL MICHAEL
(He who is like God)

Archangel Michael is the Angel of Protection. He is a large Angel who is often depicted slaying a demon with his mighty sword. Call upon this Archangel as a strong protector and support system. Archangel Michael is one of the most popular Angels within several spiritual and religious traditions. Angels and Archangels are of the spiritual realm and can be in more than one place at once so asking them to help your friends and family is okay.

His chief functions include ridding the world of fear and toxic energies and assisting with your career and purpose. Finding meaning or purpose in your life is another task assigned to Michael. He can provide you with signs or give you direction regarding your career and assist you in taking the next steps. Angels are here to offer you guidance and protection. Only you can lead and direct your own life. However, you can ask Archangel Michael to help you discover your passions and connect them with a fulfilling career that provides for all of your material needs.

Communicating your needs with Archangel Michael and being open to receiving his guidance and protection can help you live your life for the highest and best good.

If you notice sparks of bright blue or purple, Michael is probably showing his presence as he assists you in your earthly endeavors. Calling upon Angels for home or personal protection is simple and easy to do. Archangel Michael's purpose is to protect the Earth from lower energies. Call upon Michael to escort lower energies or entities to the divine light for transmutation and purification. You can ask him to help you feel safe and replace any sense of fear with love. By removing fears and negative thinking, Archangel Michael can help boost your confidence and courage. This can work during an actual time you feel threatened or when you just need some extra faith and increase in self-esteem to perform a task or for emotional support.

Archangel Michael is often utilized during automatic writing because of his strong presence and powerful messages. Channeled or automatic writing is a tool that allows you to connect with your Higher Self, Angels, or other spirit guides. Through a process of writing questions and receiving answers, you can gain insight about life areas that are important to you.

Archangel Michael Prayer

Please surround me and my loved ones. Protect us, our homes, vehicles, and valuables so that no harm may come to us. Help me to clarify my life's purpose and give me direction so that I may be of service to others every day. For this I am so grateful. Amen.

ARCHANGEL METATRON

Metatron is a powerful angel who teaches people how to use their spiritual power for good while he records their choices in the universe's great archive known either as God's Book of Life or the Akashic Record. Some believers say that Metatron is one of only two angels who was first a human being (the prophet Enoch from the Torah and the Bible) before ascending to heaven and becoming an angel (the other is Archangel Sandalphon). Metatron's experience living on Earth as a person gives him a special ability to relate to people who want to connect with him. Metatron is the twin guardian of the Tree of Life. Through geometry he reveals our connection with all life.

He assists us with our journey to complete unity and our Higher Self.

Ask Metatron for help when you have lost your connection to source, God. Call upon Metatron when you want to cleanse your chakras, and when you need help with organization.

Archangel Metatron Prayer

Archangel Metatron connect me with all that there is above. Please be with me as I journey to a Higher Self. Through my crown chakra I feel my connection with all. For this I am so grateful Amen.

CHAPTER 6
CUTTING THE TIES THAT BIND

Releasing the energy of psychic and emotional contracts with another not only helps us to regain our psychic energy but it frees us and those that we are connected with to heal and live better lives. The kind of emotional energy behind these contracts usually relate to the chakra they hook into. These attachments are known as etheric cords and they are energy links, a bit like tubes, that can form between two people. These tubes extend from chakra to chakra, depending on the type of attachment formed. Energy moves along these tubes between two people, sometimes draining from one toward the other or vice versa. You can have many of these cords attached to you at the one time. Unfortunately, this means that others can access your energy field (unconsciously, of course), which is not good news for you. If the other person is having a bit of a difficult time, they can draw upon your energy supply for their own needs, leaving you feeling tired and drained. But the good news is you can release these cords.

Please be assured that cutting these cords in no way diminishes your relationships with others. You are not releasing the love and positive feelings. Your emotional and intuitive connection will still be the same; this just releases the dysfunctional energy drain that can be a part of close relationships. You can set the intention beforehand of cutting only those cords that prevent you from experiencing your greatest joy, happiness and optimum health.

There are conscious agreements and subconscious agreements. The bonds created by these agreements may be negative or positive. They all leave their mark in that they control how we respond in life which affects each chakra body. A conscious agreement could simply be based on a mutual exchange and once completed each person would withdraw their energy. Examples of this would be the exchange of doing the dishes because someone else has made dinner, or receiving a product in exchange for money. The difference between the conscious and subconscious is that subconscious ties and psychic agreements are made wherever there are strong emotions. We hold onto those emotions and expectations and become held by the object of those feelings. For instance, when we speak of "being hooked," or "being a part of another," we're actually referring to the allowance of another's psychic cords to reach into us. If we can be emotionally triggered by a person, present or not, we are still holding that energetic tie. Unhealthy cords drain vital energy, and we refer to those on the other side of those cords as psychic vampires. Just think of all the people you may be sharing your space with that you have had strong emotions over.

Removing energy ties does not cut off unconditional love. So often, however, "love" becomes a medium for control. In the name of "love" we allow others to use and abuse us. The lack of awareness in our boundaries can lead us to give away small pieces of ourselves. When we cut negative cords we take back our power and feel much better mentally, spiritually, physically and emotionally.

Emotions play a large role in our lives. If we are not in touch with our inner selves and do not know how to set boundaries we can get stuck in all sorts of confusing and destructive energy combinations. One such example would be a mother whose adult son is addicted to drugs and alcohol. As a mother she feels responsible for his addiction because of his birth defect that caused major surgeries in his youth. Through her own guilt she overcompensates her parental care. Deep down she feels that cutting her emotional ties with her son would be cutting off the support she feels he needs to finally grow up. This situation is a perfect example of a woman not being in touch with her true feelings. Because of her own co-dependent pattern of her needing her son to need her, she confuses love with support. We can still love someone, but we must have firm boundaries in place so that we can offer the support that is best needed and still maintain our true selves.

Many times a member of a family functions as an emotional dumpster or mediator for the parents or other siblings. There is often one of these members in each family unit. This pattern most likely stems from childhood when emotions and problems were taken on by one person to fix the negativity or dysfunction. Contracts can be between ex-lovers, parents and children, and friends, to name a few. When there is a contract, there is a lingering feeling of unfinished business or a feeling that something has to happen to be done. This only keeps us hooked and does not allow us to function in our full power because our energy is extended to feed someone else. Some examples of these types of contracts include:

1. As the oldest child you put your needs last by putting the youngest sibling's emotional and physical needs before your own.

2. As a middle child, you put your needs in the background for the sibling who needs the most care.

3. A child acts as a surrogate wife or husband and absorber of the father's or mothers emotional and sexual energies when parental relations are strained. This occurs when the mother or father withdraws her/his sex or in divorce. This allows the father or mother to hook into second chakra energy whenever he/she feels the need.

4. Giving away energy due to guilt for being a burden to parents and therefore take on their emotions and pain.

5. You absorb other's anger, without permission to feel your own.

How to Clear the Chakra System

Part of our healing process involves letting go of all things that do not support our path to a healthy, emotional, vibrant life. This is why we periodically need to cleanse the chakras of things which have caused energy blockages in our etheric (energetic) body. In order to restore our individual power we must eliminate these destructive attachments and cut off the energy of those who support that negative state. We do this first through the etheric body where the energy problems exist.

Our chakras can be affected by past life contracts that recycle old problems. We may be affected by someone's mere presence. These contracts with others reinforce and hold us in our emotionally conditioned habits. Our chakras are energy transmitters and receiving stations that translate energy into messages or feelings. How we metabolize these energies determines whether they are received subconsciously or in an aware state. Awareness is an acute sensitivity to our surroundings. If we are attuned to our body sensations we can feel the pull of these subtle shifts energetically in a particular chakra in the area of our body that it resides, before they are assimilated into feelings, such as negative mood states. The ability to identify the area of the energy hooks in the body, gives us clues about the nature of the issue, contract or the depth that they have created disease in the body.

How to Identify the Chakra to be Cleared:

1. The root chakra is concerned with primordial energy for survival. Hooks in this chakra relate to insecurity and dependency through someone else's existence. We look to the first chakra when there are addictions and compulsions; sexual dysfunctions (physical, behavioral and emotional); family dysfunction; gender role confusion; child abuse issues; reproductive issues; career and finance issues; or housing, food and basic needs issues.

2. Naval chakra energy may be linked with the loss of a child or suppression of the creative life force, whether in birthing or general creativity. Hooks in this area create women's issues such as infertility, PMS, Candida, ovarian cysts and tumors, general reproductive disorders, and uterine problems. The second chakra also relates to childhood issues, co-dependency that takes on or stores other's feelings, and creative blocks that affect our right to feel. All issues relating to stored, stagnant, or

unexpressed emotions from self and others reside here. Colitis and diverticulitis are often symptoms of blocked creative energies.

3. Solar plexus chakra hooks relate to power issues and self-control issues affecting our right to act. Power issues, feelings of confusion or craziness, weight issues, digestive and metabolic disorders, and a whole range of organ disorders that complement different issues in the use of power.

4. Heart chakra hooks relate to someone that has affected our ability to love openly and unconditionally, affecting our right to love and be loved. Co-dependency and care through the heart chakra mix up love with power needs. Relationship problems, sleeping disorders, lung related problems and breast cancer are often symptomatic of long term invasion.

5. Throat chakra hooks are commonly associated with someone stifling our ability to communicate or to speak our truth. Any disorders that affects the throat area, jaw, thymus may be rooted in hooks here. So might the inability to be clear as in a "no" or "yes", victimization

from non-assertion, and issues of under or over responsibility.

6. Third eye chakra hooks us into illusion, the buying into of someone else's dream or paradigm structure, affecting our right to see truth. Obstruction produces: growth and development issues; adolescent issues; difficulty planning for the future; eyesight problems; headaches in the brow from mental or visual over-exertion or under-exertion; and glandular or endocrine issues that lead to hormonal imbalances.

7. The crown chakra may be blocked by someone we had a spiritual connection with, but whose ego is holding us back affecting our right to know. Hooks and blockages in the crown include: imbalance of any type that may be felt as disassociation, headaches, dizziness or lightheadedness; lack of self-understanding; lack of direction; immune system disorders; bone disorders; cancer; nervous system disorders and all problems relating to the pineal gland (which operates as the psychic attunement and purpose center and as an immune system regulator); learning disorders; schizophrenia; multiple personality disorder; and major depression.

The ties or the psychic cords that bind us in agreements exist on the subtle level even though we feel them on the physical level through our emotional body. For instance, we experience feelings and emotions in various parts of our bodies. Fear is clutched within our gut, our stomachs sink in disappointment, our heart gets heavy, we feel a pain in the neck, our throat wells up that we cannot speak, or our heads may spin with confusion.

Communication at this level does not require words. What is not felt empathically or intuitively is often intellectually understood via memory. It is at this level that we ignore our body's inner directive of alarm and conceal our emotions in game playing that wreaks emotional havoc within ourselves and others that leaves us most susceptible to psychic invasion where attachments form.

Cords are condensed, tentacle-like energies that function like an energetic umbilical cord in the same way that a fetus is fed and connected to the mother on the physical level. However, the cords that connect an infant's root chakra to its mother's root chakra help the infant to feel grounded and safe, which is a necessary and basic right of the infant. The cord that connects the infant's heart chakra to the mother's heart chakra allows the infant to bond with the mother on a soul level. In sexual relationships, lovers are usually connected between the heart and root chakras for exchanging love, sexual energy and soul bonding. These are healthy symbiotic relationships, although all bonds exchanged are not essentially healthy. Exchanging energy through the heart chakra allows us to bond without creating codependence. It is through the heart that we have authentic meaningful connection, as it bridges the reality of the lower chakras with the reality of the higher chakras.

We are usually unaware of the cords we have received or given to others. But a good indication of an unhealthy cord is the feeling of being drained in the presence of a parent, sibling or someone else whose emotions we feel inside our self. This always involves some form of power struggle. We can especially see this in the imbalance of sexual relationships where the cords are connected between the root and the solar plexus.

When removing these cords it must be done very gently rather than yanked out, which could create tears in the etheric body and much damage to the chakras. Yanking the cords may also elicit a reaction from the other person by letting the other person know that you are withdrawing the feeding cord. This is undesirable because it can cause the other person to retaliate psychically. We know that we are corded when we feel a "buzzy" or "tingly" energy, or a more concentrated or intense energy along our chakras that may feel thick and heavy. Essentially, energy that is denser than the rest of the aura that has well defined boundaries and that extends arms-length beyond the aura's outer edge is a cord. Follow the technique below to free yourself from these cords.

Exercise 1. Clearing the Chakras of Psychic Cords

1. Close your eyes and ground yourself as you did in Chapter 1 (White Light Prayer). Adjust your aura boundaries by imagining your entire aura encased in a protective bubble (hold your arms outstretched from your body, this is how far in all directions you want to envision your aura being in a protective bubble). If you like, before you start, you can call on Archangel Michael to assist you with this cord cutting exercise. Just ask him to come, and he will be there. There are no fancy words necessary. And remember to thank him when you are done!

2. Imagine a golden sun emanating golden light into your crown chakra and down to the top of your throat chakra, then out the little channels that go down throughout the top of your shoulders, down your arms and out of your palm chakras.

3. Visualizing the golden light, use it to flush this healing channel out for 30 seconds. You will actually feel the energy moving through your palms.

4. Now very slowly move either hand through your aura keeping it close to the front of your body.

5. Scan the front of your body beginning at your head, face and neck, moving down to your chest, solar plexus, abdomen and groin area in succession. You should be able to feel the subtle changes of your energy field.

6. Search for sensations that feel tingly or denser than the rest of your aura. If these spots do not reach to the aura's outer edge, the energy is not likely a cord.

7. Once a cord has been located, attempt to identify the person with whom you are corded. Often, the identity is obvious by the feeling of the cord. If uncertain, say the

name aloud of the person you believe it to be while at the same time keeping your hand on the cord. It will respond by changing its vibration in some way (stronger or hotter). If there is no response, it may be someone that you have not spoken to for years as in the case of an ex-spouse, lover or friend.

8. Now bring your hand to the place of your body where the cord connects and, while running the cosmic gold light through your palms, gently pry the cord loose around the edges. Pull the cord's roots little by little until it is freed from your body.

9. Place the end of the cord you have just pulled out into a rose and blow it up with the cord inside. See the cord sizzling into nothingness.

10. Now fill the hole of the pulled cord with golden light running through your hands all the way from your body to the outer edges of your aura.

11. Cords in the back tend to be more covert, subconscious, and controlling than in the front. Now imagine your backside reflected in a mirror onto your minds screen. Hurl a ball of purple light against it with

the intent of illuminating any cord in your back that needs to be cleared.

12. After locating the cord repeat steps 7-9, though you will have to visualize putting the cord into a rose and blowing it up in your mind's eye. Seal the hole visually on your mind's screen.

13. Reground yourself if necessary and then open your eyes.

When you find a cord in the same place over and over again, or if it pops back in as soon as you try to push it out it reflects a deeply held belief or contract with the other person cording you. Clear the beliefs by visualizing the word "cancelled" across the contract and burn it, then clear the cord again. For psychically persistent individuals, place a rose outside the aura with the persons face in it with a "NO Trespassing Sign." Replace the rose daily until there is no longer a need for it.

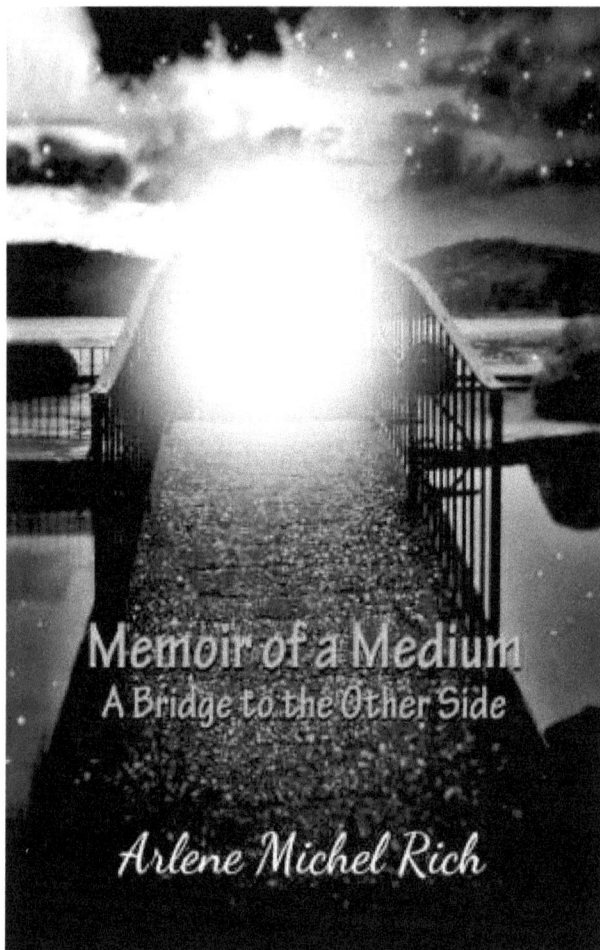

Memoir of a Medium
A Bridge to the Other Side

Arlene Michel Rich

CHAPTER 7
INTRODUCTION TO MEDIUMSHIP

When most people seek out a medium, they usually have one pressing question, "is my loved one okay?" Always, the answer is YES! It is so difficult for us to understand that all the pressures, the pain and the density of being in a body go away for people when they die. I have never done a Mediumship reading for someone who has held on to physical pain. Moving past the body allows a soul to be free of the physical issues that may have been a part of their existence on earth.

Every Medium has different experiences and even different techniques. I would like to share with you some of my experiences to help you perhaps find a way to connect with your loved ones in your own way.

For me, when I am "tuning in" to someone's energy field, if someone has recently passed, that person is very easy for me to connect with. Their Spirit is usually hovering very close. I've heard it said that you are unable to connect with a Spirit right after they pass. I have found this not to be true. There have been numerous occasions where Spirit came through while they were making their transition or at their own wake or funeral. I feel it is really about paying attention to the signs Spirit is giving to us.

Sometimes the soul of the person who has died seems to be working on resolving issues that perhaps were left undone on Earth. For example, if someone dies and there are unresolved issues with anger, the departed soul will work from the other side trying to make amends or assure the people left behind that the anger is gone and forgiveness needs to take place.

Only Pure Unconditional Love Remains

When issues seem to be blocking the person left behind from moving forward, there is usually a deep sense of urgency to resolve the issue. The crossed-over loved one is anxious for the ones left behind to move forward and finish their grief and sorrow. I have never connected with a crossed-over love one who has held on to anger or resentment. These energies do not seem to cross the barrier into the "other side". In fact, one of the reasons why I enjoy being a medium so much is that I get to experience love from the other side in a way that we seem to not be able to experience on the earthly plane. Truly, when someone crosses over, only pure unconditional love remains.

Every living person has access to communicating with those who have crossed over through death. Some have more ability than others. Some people are more naturally gifted at sports or art, while the rest of us have to work at it. The same applies to mediums.

Mediumship is a way of helping someone to recover from the death of a loved one. The pain of losing someone becomes exaggerated when nothing is known of their whereabouts or it is assumed that person is perhaps lost or alone. A medium's job is one of comfort but also responsibility. For many people to be a medium is not something they choose, it is something that just happened to them. As was the case with me when I was nine and Grandma passed. One day, they became aware of a presence beyond their own. This feeling does not leave you through your life, it increases as you mature. When you are uncertain and afraid of these experiences they become increasingly uncomfortable until you learn how to utilize them for your own good and that of others. Remain Calm... and ask questions.

How Spirit Communicates

Let go of expectations of how Spirit communicates. If you are seeking to connect with a crossed-over loved one, let go of all your preconceived ideas about how you think your experience or your communication should look like. You are probably connecting with your loved one just fine. You just may be doubting your experience.

Messages from Spirit can be received in all sorts of forms. Often through impulses (the hairs on your arm or neck stand up, a knowing, visions (clairvoyance) or through verbal communication that takes place in the mind. It is rare, and not necessary for Spirit to manifest in a physical form to communicate. Why appear in person when you can make a phone call to achieve the same effect? It can be a subtle feeling to something that is extremely real. Spirit will make their presence known through several methods often depending on their ability to communicate. A person who in life was not very good at communicating will often be similar in Spirit; if they were chatty in life they are likely to be the same in death. One of the methods they will use and one it is likely you are familiar with, is that of seeing things out of the corner of your eye or feeling that someone is there. The feeling can also extend to an awareness of being watched or sudden changes in body or room temperature (hot flashes aside). One of the more advanced methods and one that will occur when in a quiet space is communication in your mind. This is different from your own head talk. The communication will often be accompanied by visions (clairvoyance) as the Spirit attempts to show you what they wish for you to see. This form of communication may be through symbols to interpret rather than actual situations or places. When they wish to use words to communicate there will often be a short delay, much like how long distance phone calls were before satellite. If a Spirit wishes to make its' presence known through a physical appearance this can initially be scary if you are not used to it. That is why Spirit may not wish to make a physical presence (unless absolutely necessary) because it is hard work for them to reduce themselves into physical matter. Unless they are an earth bound or recently passed Spirit, it is unlikely you will see Spirit with your eyes unless you are vibrating at a speed close to their own (experienced mediums). If they do choose to appear physically to you, they will communicate telepathically or will mime what they want to say.

Different mouls seem to have different skill levels of communication. Sometimes I will encounter a Soul who just loves to talk and can communicate quite clearly. The most common way that crossed-over loved ones seem to communicate is through working in dream-time. I tell my students and clients that if they have a dream in which they see and talk to their loved one and they can recall every detail, a week, a month and years later, that it was a visitation from their loved one and not just a lovely dream. Be grateful if you have these kinds of communication.

Most Spirits tell me that they talk to their loved ones all the time but their loved ones just don't listen. My experience is that they can talk to us sometimes in our head. You may actually hear your loved ones voice in your head, but then discount it or think you are experiencing wishful thinking. Trust yourself and what you are experiencing. If you are hearing a loved-one in your head, you probably really are!

Spirit will start a communication in several different ways. The most common seems to be feelings through your body. The Spirit will often first wish to communicate to you how they died. They may show it as a physical sensation in the body, a milder version of what they experienced when they died. What they show you in your own body does not usually hurt, but is often up to you to interpret. If the information is not clear, it is then necessary to ask them to clarify what they are trying to say. Following a feeling of how they died they will speak through thoughts in the mind or repeat their name over and over again. If the medium is not experienced in receiving messages it is likely they will dismiss them as their own thoughts or imagination. This will frustrate the Spirit who will try and push their way in further. If it is in a group (psychic circle) the Spirit will be likely to then move to someone more receptive.

Facts about Mediumship to be Aware Of

If Spirit has been trying for any length of time to get through to a loved one they will have a sense of relief once they do get through. Similar to when you try to speak to a friend who has been ignoring you, to get acknowledgement. The relief for Spirit is often overwhelming. Spirit, without their physical bodies find it difficult to release emotion. The medium's job may be to release that emotion for them. If this should happen the medium may begin to cry or experience the Spirit's upset. Don't be alarmed just know this is temporary and calmly allow the feeling to pass through the body. Once the Spirit has said what it needs to, the connection will weaken and disappear. I often feel the emotion of the Spirit so strongly that I cry with my clients. I always have a box of tissues on hand for this reason. Crying is an emotional release and is good for everyone, so don't feel self-conscious.

Earthbound Spirits are also known as ghosts. A ghost is the energy, soul or personality of a person who has died and is somehow stuck between this plane of existence and the next. Mostly, these Spirits do not know they are dead. They may have died under traumatic, unusual or highly emotional circumstances. Time is not the same in the Spirit world. Mediums can experience Spirits in many ways: through clear sight-apparitions ESP, the sixth sense (clairvoyance), sounds and voices (clairaudience), smell (fragrances or odors), touch - and sometimes they can just be sensed and felt (clairsentience).

Unexpected Deaths

Sometimes, if someone has died unexpectedly or suddenly, there is a little bit of shock that a Soul can experience. I don't encounter this often, but when I do, I can call on the Soul's family members who have passed and Archangel Michael to help the soul adjust to being on the other side. I had many souls from 9/11 who needed help crossing over and help understanding that they were not still on the earth plane.

Once when I was doing a reading for a police detective, a New York City transit cop came through. He had passed on 9/11 and because he felt comfortable with another man in blue he came into this gentlemen's reading. The detective did not know him personally. After the detective left I helped the transit policeman cross over; by directing him to go to the light where others would be waiting for him.

There are strictly two types of earthbound Spirits - lost ones and bad ones. I use the term bad but I could also say lesser good. Those we would not have wanted to associate with on the earth plane if we had a choice! If you should come across an earthbound Spirit you should immediately be able to tell if they are lost.

Lost earthbound Spirits (those that have died suddenly) will be wandering around aware of the physical world but unable to get through, caught between two worlds, one they are reluctant to leave and one they are afraid to enter. Lost Spirits should be encouraged to go 'towards the light'. They will understand this message and an opening will occur for them to pass through. Spirits can also be earthbound due to a loved one's reluctance to let them go, if this is the case they should be encouraged to go towards the light. Explain how they will be met by loved ones and they are not alone.

People have asked me if "bad" Spirits come through. Not for me. I always say a prayer before each reading that it is for the client's highest good and that only Spirits of a higher vibration come through. In cases where clients say their homes are haunted or even their place of business I recommend that a house clearing and blessing be performed. The Spirit is then sent to the light.

What is a Haunting?

A haunting is a kind of "recording" of a past event on an environment, such as a house, building or a battlefield. These recordings play back, over and over in a kind of loop - always the same, like a film or video. They are not able to communicate with us. It would be like talking to your television and expecting an answer. They are usually associated with a traumatic event or very strong emotional upheaval.

Bad earthbound Spirits will often show as poltergeists, bad smells, and deep feelings of unease. They will be the ones who try to trick and frighten the living. It is often the case though, that your own Spirit guide and Angel will protect you from bad Spirits. So remember to call them in! I call upon Archangel Michael, the protector Angel to surround me in his protection and also to lead the earthbound Spirit to the light. If you come across a bad earthbound Spirit the best thing to do is remain calm. Call to your Spirit guides and guardian Angel. You do this by asking and trusting that they are going to be there. Be firm and tell the Spirit clearly to leave your presence. Remember you are in charge!

Receiving Messages

To be an effective medium it is necessary to prepare. Even if you find it very easy to communicate with Spirit you do have to be responsible about yourself and the Spirit you are communicating with. That sensitivity no matter what your level as a medium has to be protected. It takes a lot of psychic energy to maintain contact with those who have passed over.

Many mediums who are very good find themselves getting very tired. Even mediums who have years of experience find themselves getting tired and needing lengthy periods of mental rest. Some mediums can go on forever, appearing to be energized rather than tired after a reading (this happens to me, I feel like the energizer bunny!).

Why Mediums Get Tired

When a medium is channeling they receive and transmute psychic energy. This psychic energy can get stuck in the chakras if they are not cleansed, often leading to physical complaints for the medium. They can get stuck with some of the energy of the communicating Spirit or with the energy of the person they are communicating for. This energy can get trapped in the

112

solar plexus. To prevent this from happening, ALWAYS thank Spirit (dead people) for their presence when done with the communication and clear any energies that are no longer productive for the Spirit or humans present to be taken at the point of their departure. I also sage after each session.

Be Mindful to Use the Earth Energy

The Earth energy is there to be used. It is what we all walk around on but rarely tap into. It is an extremely powerful energy that tends to be forgotten about. We have chakras on the bottom of our feet, when exposed to the Earth energy the feet will absorb through the chakras, energizing the system. If a medium uses the earth energy when channeling they will maintain contact longer and often clearer than they would if they were not using it. You may wish to remove your shoes when making contact. The Earth energy can be tapped into simply by drawing it up (in the mind) through the bottom of the feet, up the legs and into the solar plexus.

Channel the Energy

Many mediums look very healthy from the chest up. They often have faces younger than their years. This is because the channeling of 'light' on a consistent basis will help to rejuvenate the chakras keeping them healthy. However, many mediums only use the upper chakras (crown, third eye, throat, and heart chakras) to channel information, often forgetting about the ones further down the body. The chakras on the upper body therefore gather pace while the lower ones get progressively slower. The lower part of the body then becomes sluggish; the Medium experiencing leg, and hip problems and the lower half of the body starts to gather weight. However, if the medium draws up the earth energy through the feet into the solar plexus and draws down energy from the upper body chakras to meet with the earth energy in the solar plexus they become energized during mediumship readings (I'm now releasing any excess weight; I put it out to the universe!).

Work on Your Baggage! (we ALL have some)

It is not enough on a spiritual level to simply live a good life and be a nice person to evolve as far you can on the earth plane. Although it does help! To evolve psychically it is necessary to deal with your baggage. Every person has baggage! No one gets away with it! I believe if we did not have any baggage to overcome and learn from we would not be here.

Our soul would have little to learn if we were perfect. However, most people go through life burying their baggage until the day they die. If a Medium chose to bury things they will soon become tired and exhausted. Perhaps even frightened of their work, eventually shutting their ability down. If a person is willing to face and deal with their inner fears, they will gain an ability to 'see' more clearly. They will be able to give readings that are free of their own slant on matters. Spirit would also then find it is easier to connect. Imagine a medium as a light bulb in a sea of lights. If the bulb is burning very brightly Spirit can spot the light very easily. Remember to shine your own light!

Do Not Hold on to Grief

The more grief a family feels, the harder it is for a soul to progress to the next level. When we deny our grief, the Soul gets trapped trying to make things better. This is so true when I am working with children who have died. Children always tell me to tell their parents to stop crying and to enjoy their own lives. They want their parents to know they have not left them and that they are still a part of the family, just in a different form. Children seem to stay in their parent's energy fields for a long time and almost seem to "grow up" next to their parents even though they are no longer here. As soon as we begin to resolve our grief, the soul can then go on to the next level of their development.

People always ask me "are my loved ones ok?" Yes, they are better than okay. They are Spirit and therefore do not have the limitations of this physical body any longer. If they had major issues in this lifetime, perhaps they are continuing to learn on the other side. If we don't learn the lesson we were brought here to experience we are destined to repeat it till we get it right. Your loved ones have not left you so they do not miss you. The only difference is now you must learn how to communicate differently. It's like you speak two different languages. With practice you will learn what they are saying.

Do our Pets Meet us in Heaven?

Pets do come through in readings as well their human counterparts. We can communicate with our pets in Spirit. If you have a living pet, do you ever notice this pet staring at or chasing some invisible object? Watch closely, and you will be able to tell that they are still playing with their passed-on friend. Animals don't think, they just react. They "see" and "sense" the pet in Spirit.

Animals also see human Spirits. They don't try and reason why it is impossible to see Spirit. They just "know" and experience. We can learn a lot from our furry friends. Pets seem to be able to connect better than humans. Many souls will show me images of dogs or cats. Pay attention to your animals. They can perceive energy in a way that we can't sometimes.

Allow me to tell you about our little Rosie who stole everyone's heart. We adopted Rosie when she was ten months old. Rosie is an English Cocker Spaniel with the most beautiful loving brown eyes. Over the years everyone who ever pet her commented on how silky and beautiful her coat was, but it is the love that she exuded in those eyes that captivated all who met her.

Rosie was part of our family for almost sixteen years. People would call me Rosie's mom. They may not have remembered my name but they remembered hers!

When it was time for her to leave this lifetime it was very emotional for everyone. We knew that we had to make the decision to let her go in peace and dignity and not to have her suffer anymore. The day we took her to the vet I held her and told her how much we loved her and how much happiness she had brought to our family and everyone's lives she touched. I held her in my arms when she took her last breath.

Afterwards I was driving to meet my friend at the park to walk. I had the car radio on. I asked God to give me a sign that Rosie was okay now. As a spiritual medium I have brought through for my clients many animals that have crossed over. I immediately heard a voice say turn on your CD. Player. I have a ten-CD changer that I do not use regularly. The answer came in these words as a direct response to my question, "I'll walk with God from this day on. There is no death though eyes grow dim, there is no fear when I'm near to him" Then in my mind's eye I "saw" Rosie as a young ten-month-old frolicking in a beautiful meadow. She was very happy and healthy again!

I was amazed!!! This was not a CD I had played even in the last year, nor is that the first song on the CD, nor were they the first words of the song! What a gift I had been given.

When I met my friend at the park I was crying but not tears of sorrow, tears of gratitude that I had my answer. Rosie was "home" being well taken care of once again. The signs didn't end there. As we were walking we saw a puppy exactly like Rosie, a Black English Cocker Spaniel about ten months old! This color and type of dog is rare to see! I had been given another symbol just to make certain I knew she was okay. I started laughing through my tears and looked up to the sky and said "thanks God! Thank you for answering my prayers."

It was such a blessing to receive these messages for myself and my family. Rosie has been gone physically from my life for years now but she is still very much a part of my life. I can tell by our other dogs - especially Remi who was Rosie's pal for 5 ½ years - that she comes to visit! I hope by telling Rosie's story that it brings comfort to everyone who has ever loved and had to let go of their beloved pet. You will be with them again

So to sum it all up for you now, the different ways you know you've connected with Spirit are:

The feeling- when you are in contact with Spirit you will feel spiritually uplifted, peaceful, joyful and whole.

The Inner Knowingness – A sense of Knowing, without knowing how you know it- is intuition.

The Voice – The voice of Spirit is normal and natural without theatrics! It may be French or Arabic but always calm.

The Quality –the quality of the message you receive is uplifting, positive and LOVING.
Test again the feeling you have after the message is given. What was the message? Is it about forgiveness? Love? HOW do YOU FEEL? This is the true test of whether you communicated with Spirit either directly on your own or through a medium. Remember, trust what you are getting, your own intuition will guide you.

Exercise 1: Automatic writing

It is very easy to connect with Spirit through channeled writing. Simply write a question for your loved one on paper. If you have a picture of them, hold it and look at their eyes, the window to the Soul. You can even write them a letter if you want to. Once you are done with your writing, close your eyes, take a few deep breaths and ask that you be connected with your loved one.

As soon as you feel ready write what you think the answer would be to your question or your letter.

If you are deeply skeptical do this anyway, you may never feel "ready". Just write what comes into your head. You may find that as you continue to write, the words come faster and even the tone of voice of your words may change. This is just your loved one coming through for you!

The biggest block to connecting with a crossed-over loved one is skepticism. We doubt so many of our divine messages because they don't happen the way we think they should. Let go of your doubt and just play. If you think you can't connect with a departed one, imagine what it would be like if you could, and see what happens.

Losing a loved one can be a devastating experience. Allow yourself to feel your grief and your sorrow. The more you allow for your sadness, the more quickly you can move past it. When my clients are not allowing their sadness, the pain and the grief goes on much longer and can even manifest in physical illness. As hard as it is, let it go. It has been my experience that time does truly heal the pain and that only the love remains. Our departed loved ones encourage us to release our grief. Completing our grief sets us and them free. It makes room for more love into our lives. Talk about them, honor them and send them love. They are truly right there with you! We are really never alone.

After our loved ones cross over, they are very anxious to let us know they are okay and are aware of what is going on in our lives. They will often give us signs that we cannot ignore. The person who is given the sign usually senses that he or she is receiving a message from the other side. I always tell my clients to look for signs, to be aware and use all of their senses! A thorough listing of the signs our loved ones may give us are included in Appendix I: Psychic Symbol Glossary. They may place common objects such as feathers or coins in our path. Our loved ones like to place things over and over again in our path that were significant to them. I have had clients come to me who have had jars filled with feathers, coins, and objects they have found in the most unusual places. I find feathers in very unusual places as well, and I have also found pennies in unusual spots. Once when I was traveling down my road coming back from church I had my sun roof open. A penny came in through the roof. This truly was a penny from heaven, and at church we had sung that song, "Pennies from Heaven!" Confirmation for sure.

They can come through as an animal. Our loved ones are able to use their energy to go inside of an animal, such as a butterfly, ladybug, bird, or dragonfly. It does NOT mean that your loved one has reincarnated as an animal. They are merely using the animal for a brief time to communicate their presence to you. The animal does something it usually would not do, such as land on us. When my father passed there was a huge beautiful moth that was at my front door. It stayed there for days. I would go out onto the front porch and sit and talk with it. I even lightly touched it and it did not fly away.

They may give off fragrances. We can often tell our deceased loved ones are around us when we smell their perfume, flowers, cigar or cigarette smoke, or any other familiar smell they had. There is usually no logical explanation of why the smell is there. Sometimes when my father is near I smell Old Spice or if it is my father-in-law I smell cherry pipe tobacco. When I smell or see a rose I think of my mother or Nana who are both named Rose.

They make songs come on at the perfect time. We know they are around when their favorite songs come on at the right time with the exact words we need to hear. Often the same song is played in many different places.

They come to us in dreams. One of the easiest ways for them to come through to us is in our dreams. All we need to do is to ask them to come, and they *will*. However, we should ask them to wake us up after they come, or else we will not remember the dream. A dream that is a true visitation will be very peaceful and we will *know* it is truly our loved one. We will remember this type of dream in detail many years later. Alternately, a subconscious dream may be frightening or feel bad, or may be forgotten quickly. This type of dream is *not* your loved one.

They show us the same numbers over and over. They love to give us numbers that are relevant to them or you, such as birthdates, anniversaries – or repeating numbers, such as 1111, 2222, 3333, etc. These numbers may appear on clocks, billboards, or any other familiar place.

They allow us to feel peaceful for no reason. When our loved ones are in the room, they usually make us feel so loved and at peace. It usually happens at the most unsuspecting time, so there is no logical explanation for our sudden bliss. They place thoughts in our head. Because they are in Spirit form, our loved ones don't have an audible voice. Therefore, they give us messages telepathically. Pay attention to thoughts that just "pop" into your head. We can tell the difference between our thoughts and theirs by backtracking our thoughts. If you can find the thought that triggered the thought of your loved one, it is probably *your* thought. If something your loved one would say just *pops* in your head for no reason, it is probably him or her speaking directly to you!

They love to play with electricity. They turn electricity on and off. They like to flicker lights, turn the television and radio on and off, and make appliances beep for no apparent reason. Yesterday while sitting at my computer

I was drawn to a fairy on a shelf that was my sister-in-law's. She passed almost four years ago. I acknowledged her by speaking to her out loud. Just then, the CD player slot opened on my laptop. I had not been playing any music so I just closed it. A minute later it opened again. I stopped what I was doing and continued to "speak" with her. When we were finished with our conversation my twin brother who was married to her called "out of the blue" just to say hello.

They make buzzing noises in our ears. Because our loved ones speak to us on a different, higher frequency, we may hear ringing in our ears when they are trying to get our attention. This is a sign telling you to listen to what they are saying.

The list goes on and on, but these are the most common ways they let us know they are around. If you haven't received any of these signs, simply *ask* your loved ones to come to you to let you know they are okay. Be patient and persistent, and I promise that they *will* give you the signs you have always wanted. They really are okay and want you to be too!

Exercise 2: Direct Communication

Set your intention! Sit quietly in an upright position with feet on the floor. Do not cross your arms, legs, ankle, or anything else. In your mind, surround yourself in a golden bubble and say the White Light prayer or one that suits you. (Ground and Shield)

Call in your helpers, guides, call them in by name, and visualize them. Affirm in your mind you are totally protected.

If you are comfortable with this, ask for Spirit (dead people) to step forward and make their presence known to you. This may show as thoughts, seeing in your mind. You may sense you are not alone. Feel extreme cold or warmth! Fragrances, sometimes smoke if person was a smoker. Tell Spirit (in your mind) that you are new to this and ask for them to make themselves clear to you. Say you will do your best to accept their presence.

TRUST what you get! Accept rather than reject. Say Thank You and disconnect!

Join a group known as a Psychic Circle and PRACTICE!

Exercise 3: Psychometry

Take a picture you have of your loved one where you can clearly see their eyes is preferred. Hold it in your hand, connect thru their eyes, say their name, and hold an object of theirs if possible as well.

What do you feel? See the person in your mind's eye? Can you smell a scent you associate with them? Perfume, cologne, smoke? Flower? Picture them in a favorite outfit of theirs. Ask a question! Then listen for the answer.

To summarize, I suggest you become acutely AWARE of your surroundings and of how you FEEL and that you TRUST what you get. Practice, Practice, Practice...

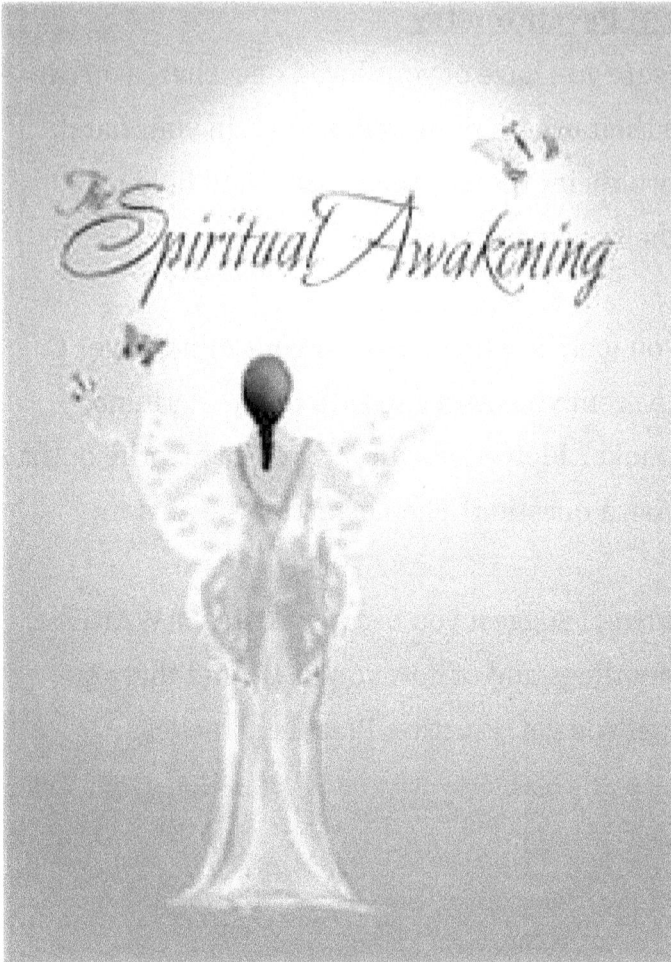
The Spiritual Awakening

CHAPTER 8
SO NOW WHAT?

My book is not intended to be the end of your education. It has only skimmed the surface of how you may refine and use your psychic abilities. I have walked this earth for many years and most of them being very aware. However, I still love to learn new ways of taping into my own abilities. Using your psychic abilities is a way of life. No longer will you be able to turn a blind eye to things. Your senses have all become acutely aware of their ability to tap into your intuition in all areas of your life, for the fullest expression of all that you are. There no longer is any situation that you cannot handle more easily and with more insight. By sensitizing yourself to always be aware of your surroundings you may now have a wealth of tools from which to draw from. You now will be able to solve problems more effortlessly and be able to see all sides of every situation by tuning into your innate abilities.

A gentle warning from me would be, do not become too impressed with yourself! I know that with these new found or increased powers it is easy to think, your all that. So what? You're a psychic, everyone is. Perhaps they have not been practicing their skills as much as you, however, they do have the same ability.

I beg you please, do not go around giving unsolicited advice announcing you're a psychic. Or worse still, do not approach someone by saying, "I'm a medium and I see your dead mother standing behind you and I want to tell you what I think she has to say!" I have seen psychics and mediums who have become quite egotistical and in doing so they may have started out with great abilities but because of their own self absorption their talent is diminished. God giveth and God can take it away! The power really remains with God, source, however you wish to say it. We are merely channels. When I say a prayer before I see a client (or do a phone session) I state I humbly will give any information I receive. I know it is NOT about me. I am grateful to have the knowledge and know how to help clarify things for people, bring them peace in situations, and help in any way I can. I truly feel I am here to help.

So here are some more exercises to enhance those abilities.

Exercise 1: Tuning in

• Close your eyes. Take three deep breaths to relax.

• Visualize the sun resting on top of your head. Visualize the number 3 in the center of the sun.

• Allow the sun to move downward through your body, warming and relaxing your body as it goes.

• Feel the warmth and relaxation.

• When the sun reaches your toes, allow it to leave them.

• Then visualize another sun, with the number 2 in the center of the sun, resting on the top of your head.

• Allow the sun number 2 to move downward through your body, warming and relaxing your body as it goes just as the other did.

• Then visualize another sun, with the number 1 in its center resting on the top of your head.

• Allow the sun number 1 to move downward through your body, warming and relaxing your body as it goes just as the other two suns did.

• Feel the total relaxation now.

• Say to yourself, "from now on all I need to do to reach this relaxed psychic level is to close my eyes and mentally count from three down to one." Open your eyes.

If you are a woman who tends to have "hot flashes" or as I like to call them "power surges" than you may substitute the word Moon and its cool imagery for the Sun.

Exercise 2: Dictionary

Hold a dictionary (or any book) on your lap. Think of ONE question. Do the exercise with the sun we just did. Then flip through the dictionary without looking. Feel when your hand should stop turning the pages. When you feel you have reached the right place, open your eyes and read. Somewhere within the definition of the word will be your answer, or a clue to your question.

More Exercises for Psychic Development with a Partner

If you are comfortable with this, hold your partner's hands or touch each other's knees.

1. Ask your partner to tell you the name of someone they know and you don't. Imagine a rose in your 3rd eye chakra. (any color rose you wish) and concentrate on their name. Is the rose opening? Closing? Blooming? Wilting? Then give what you get in a respectful loving manor.

2. Have someone sit across from you and think of a color. Have them visualize the color surrounding them. Take your hands and feel the energy around them, close your eyes and "see" what color you get and tell them.

3. Write a sentence on a piece of paper that describes someone you know well and then hand it to your partner. Run your fingers over the words to tap into the personality of the person. Are they calm, excited, outgoing, artistic? Then give what you get in a respectful, loving manor.

After each exercise switch who goes next. Some people will find it easier to "send" the information and others will be more adept at "receiving".

Remember to be gentle with yourselves. Just remember practice makes perfect and remember to have fun!

How Do You Know If It's Working?

After practicing your psychic abilities over weeks and months of meditation keep a journal of your experiences. Write down the results, writing it down will help reinforce the conscious-unconscious connection.

I hope you find this book helpful in opening to the magnificent intuitive power that is within you. Use it as a resource and continue to grow and awaken to your abilities. Keep track of your progress and if I may be of further assistance or you would like to keep in touch with me please email me at Arlene@TheSpiritualAwakening.com. If you are interested my first book, *Memoir of a Medium - A Bridge to the Other Side, it* is available through Amazon.com and Kindle, BarnesandNoble.com, Kobo.com as well as area bookstores.

Blessings,
Arlene Michel Rich

APPENDIX I
PSYCHIC SYMBOL GLOSSARY

Once you open up your life it will never be the same. Here are some common symbols and their meanings or indications:

Airplane: travel coming. Whenever I see an airplane while giving a reading I know the person will be taking a long journey, usually over a body of water.

Akashic records: time to review your life. What is your Higher purpose? The Akashic records are a record of everyone's life; a filing cabinet of every thought, action and event in a person life.

Alcohol: an indicator of too much partying; addictive behavior; out of control; diluting the truth of a situation.

Alien: something feels foreign to you; a feeling of being out of control; alienated on the outside. May indicate a Spiritual Being is bringing you a message.

Ambulance: emergency; warning of harm or injury, either bodily of emotionally. Be extra careful.

Anchor: feeling tied down; seeking a lifeline; help

Angel: This could represent your desire to become more spiritual. As an omen for the future it may mean peace may come to you. All is well; protected!

Apple: healthy living, as in an apple a day keeps the doctor away.

Ax: separation from someone or an idea; splitting up; destructive behavior.

Arrow: a straight shooter; aim for the bulls eye; go for it!

Baby: someone is pregnant or the birth of a new era.

Ball: sports; "let's play." It could also mean caution, don't drop the ball as in don't lose sight of the goal.

Basement: to a hypnotherapist this indicates the subconscious mind, what is just below the surface that you are not wanting to face.

Battery: recharge your battery. It could mean your physical energy is drained or literally your car battery needs charging.

(I once did a psychic reading and saw a car battery dead. I told the gentleman to check his battery and he ignored the warning, saying the battery was only three years old. Sure enough, a week later his battery died late one night and his wife had to bundle up the kids to go give his car a jump)

Beach: relaxation. Water symbolizes emotion, so this could indicate that perhaps you need to wash away negative emotions and rejuvenate.

Bear: protective; can be overbearing; may need to hibernate and search within. What are you unable to bear any longer?
(my totem animal is a bear, I love bears)

Boat: a cruise if it's a large ship; relaxing is indicated by a small boat. May be a warning against paddling upstream; don't rock the boat.

Book: knowledge;, a need to learn; an inquisitive mind. If closed, it may mean reluctance to change your mind. When I see a stack of books I feel the person is a teacher.

Bed: a need to rest; sometimes a means to escape and shut out the world, pull the covers over your head.

Bee: busy as a bee. A worker bee can indicate an ability to work well with others; a Queen bee can indicate a need to be in charge.

Birds: birds symbolize transcendence. Consider the type of bird that you see. A dove may mean a peaceful outcome, a raven deceit, and a peacock warns you to beware of pride.

Box: are you feeling boxed in? If it is wrapped and pretty, perhaps it is a symbol of a gift coming to you. If the lid is open, perhaps it is time for you to share your gifts with others.

Butterflies: may symbolize the spiritual transformation of the soul. Many of my clients report seeing butterflies just after the passing of a loved one.

Bridge: a transition to new things. What do you see lying beyond? Is it a happy landscape or a foreboding one? You may have some good times or difficult decisions ahead. May also indicate a connection to Spirit, as in ...*a Bridge to the Other side*!

Cake: celebration; life is sweet. Alternately, it may mean that you can't have your cake and eat it too, something has got to go.

Cards: deal the cards; play; gambling; play your cards right; keep your cards close to your vest.

Carousel: going around in circles; playtime; brass ring;, go for it.

Casket: death, the death of an idea

Castle: living like a Queen or King dominating the home; a possible move to a larger home

Cat: normally associated with female qualities; the cat may symbolize your intuition. Luck, possible good fortune; a good period ahead. A cat has nine lives so it may symbolize paying attention to dangerous situations and people who are aloof like a cat.

Caterpillar: transformation; a time for a change; beautiful things unfold

Chick/Chicken: hatching plans; don't put all your eggs in one basket; scared, or "chicken"

Cross: religious symbol; a cross to bear - burden you are carrying

Crystal Ball: seeing into the future; clairvoyance; things becoming crystal clear

Church: the sacred side of you will be of importance; religion

Clock/Watch: wake up to things around you. Time is running out. Don't miss an opportunity.

Cloud: daydreaming; a need to focus -get your head out of the clouds. A dark cloud may represent a dark, ominous situation or feeling. A light cloud may represent life is carefree.

Desk: workaholic; tied to a desk, possible change in responsibilities at work. A messy desk may indicate a need to get organized, while a neat desk may indicate organized thoughts.

Death: dreaming of your own death may symbolize a death of a relationship; you're feeling lifeless, without purpose

Dead people: may be a visit from the Other Side, if it is vivid to you days and months after seeing them it was a visitation from a loved one in Spirit. If you see other people who aren't deceased it could mean they are dead to you emotionally or it is a time for a physical.

Devil: may represent a bad idea, evil temptation, devious thinking

Diamond: wealth; engagement; strength

Diploma: graduation; acknowledgement of accomplishments; a desire for further education

Dirt: nature; grounding; Mother Earth; Gossip, as in you have the "dirt" on someone

Doctor: time for a checkup perhaps; emotional or physical illness; your own healing abilities

Dog: a loyal, friendly dog indicates you can trust that person; tail wagging, aggressive dog - be wary of the person or situation; dirty dog. It could be a dog in Spirit is connecting (I have had many dogs, cats, and other pets come through
when I do readings).

Door: if open, it may be the opening to a new area of your life; an opportunity ahead. If closed it may mean you are afraid to face something. Feeling blocked from someone or something. If locked it may mean you are shutting out the outside world, not willing to be open for fear of being hurt.

Dragon: a magical, mystical, fire breathing dragon means danger ahead. Don't get burned.

Dragonfly: connection to spirituality; a message from Spirit; the wisdom of transformation and adaptability in life; prosperity; good luck. The dragonfly is a reminder that when our deeper thoughts rise to the surface we must pay attention - there are lessons to be learned, and we are also reminded that what we think is directly proportionate to what we "see on the surface." Our thoughts (even the deeper ones that we might not be as in-touch with as we are with our conscious thoughts) are responsible for what we see in our lives - in our physical surroundings.

Drum: an individualist, moving to the beat of your own drum. Drumming circle, a journey, meditation

Eagle: majestic; powerful; a symbol of the United States. An eagle soaring above indicates an ability to see things from a distance keenly.

Ear: listen more clearly; a need to be heard; clairaudience

Envelope: communication. A white envelope may be a symbol of good news, pink could indicate a loss of job or don't push the envelope. A reminder to pay your bills.

Eraser: fresh start; clean slate; erase a person or a memory; a change is coming; time to make new plans

Eyes: sight, vision. The eyes are the windows to the soul. Open eyes indicate an ability to see things clearly. Closed eyes ask "what are you afraid to see?" May represent death or the death of a relationship. The third eye indicates clairvoyance, gifted sight, an ability to see into the future.

Faces: Images of faces are likely to appear distorted but consider the expression. Does it say something about your state of mind or remind you of someone you know? The person portrayed may have a role in your future plans.

Fairy: magical, mystical, childlike as in Tinkerbell; light hearted. May be associated with the elementals – air, fire, water, and earth.

Falcon: birds of prey, swift flight, able to change direction rapidly. Symbolizes going in for the kill, going after what you want quickly.

Family: need to communicate, reach out to family member, whether here or on the Other Side.

Faucet: cleansing. Water is emotion, letting go, cleansing the mind, body and soul.

Feather: a message from Heaven. A loved one in Spirit may be letting you know he or she is with you. A symbol Angels are watching over you. Like mindedness, as in "birds of a feather flock together." May also indicate an opportunity is coming - a feather in your cap.

Fence: separation- putting up a fence between you. A white picket fence could indicate a new home or stability in home; idyllic. On the fence - unable to make a decision

Files/File cabinet: subconscious thoughts and memories, storage - file it away till later. Akashic records: the record of everyone's life, a filing cabinet of every thought, action and event in a person's life.

Finger: depends on which finger. Pointer finger: blame - is someone pointing the finger at you? Middle Finger - screw you, telling someone off. Ring finger - commitment symbol of marriage. Pinky finger - upper class - pompous behavior. Thumb up -approval great idea or hitching a ride, need help. Thumb down - negative disapproval. Green thumb - a gardener who is good with plants or planting the seeds of growth whether plants or ideas.

Finish Line: achievement, completion of a goal

Fire: may mean things are heating up; a burning desire - a fire in your soul, passion. A need to step away from a person - playing with fire, you're going to get burned. Under fire - risk taking.

Fireplace: hearth of the home, warmth and stability. If the fireplace is decorated, it may indicate a time of year (holly would indicate Christmas). It can also be seen as an entrance into another world, the unknown.

Fireworks: what sensation is felt with it? If it is excitement, this may indicate a promotion or happy news to follow. If unease is felt, perhaps the fireworks are an argument or upheaval is present. May also be a sign of danger.

Fish: a universal symbol of fertility with the promise of personal inner growth. Superstitions say that to dream of catching a fish means that good fortune will come your way. Alternately, if something is fishy it is not legitimate. Be cautious.

Flashlight: shine your own light; brilliant ideas.

Flying: I often have dreams of flying. I feel these are when I travel to other lives and places known as astral travel. It may also represent freedom or literally you will be taking a trip.

Fork in the road: decision making time, several opportunities

Funeral: death or the death of an idea.

Garbage: garbage you need to throw out, de clutter your surroundings , let go of people who treat you like garbage.

Gate: white picket gate, new home, new opportunities, may represent passing through the gate of time to a past life.

Genie: I always think of Aladdin the genie in the bottle who grants 3 wishes, or I dream of Genie the TV show. magic, good things are possible just ask and believe!

Ghost: A ghost is the energy, soul or personality of a person who has died and is somehow stuck between this plane of existence and the next. Mostly, these spirits do not know they are dead. They may have died under traumatic, unusual or highly emotional circumstances. Right after 9/11 I had to help many spirits cross over and continue to do so. Time is not the same in the spirit world. Mediums can experience spirits in many ways: through clear sight-apparitions ESP, the sixth sense (clairvoyance), sounds and voices (clairaudience), smell (fragrances or odors), touch - and sometimes they can just be sensed and felt (clairsentience)

Gift: something pleasant coming your way. or perhaps see the gifts in others and yourself.

Glasses: a need to see things clearer, a new perspective

Graduation: higher learning achieved or a need to take more course of studies.

Grave: it may be an actual grave, someone is dying or it could symbolize the need to bury something for good.

Gun: protection, may be someone is gunning for you, your job, be weary and on guard

Hammer: something needs fixing, don't hammer away at things needlessly.

Hat: symbolizes your role in life. Perhaps a change of job or role is indicated. How many hats are you wearing?

Hawk: a keen sighted bird-Hawk eyed, with ability to fly long distances swiftly. I have had a Hawk as a totem for many years. I see them practically daily

Heart: emotional issues to deal with. broken heart-heaviness of the heart. may be a sign to get checked out physically or light hearted- being of little consequence, whimsical

Heaven: Angel or Spirit communication, getting in touch with your Higher Self. Nirvana a place of tranquility

Hell: a harsh place where the Devil lives. Everything that is negative. The absence of Light.

Horse: A horse can represent untamed emotions. Horseshoes are a symbol of luck.

Hourglass: time may be running out

Hospital: a healing is needed, or a place where nurse, Drs work, may be a calling to work in a healing field

Ice: coldness, cruel, aloof behavior. If ice is cracking can mean you are in danger-on thin ice

Island: may mean a vacation or isolating oneself

Indian: (Native American) one with nature and all things. going back to simple times. I have had many Spirit Guides show up as Indians.

Jail: punishment, a crime committed, loss of one's freedom

Judge: This could represent your conscience or a conflict with authority ahead. Don't Speed!

Jury: if facing one-you feel you are being wrongly judged, if looking towards a person you are doing the judging.

Keys: A problem will be solved and you will be opening the door to opportunity. A new home or car perhaps.

King: male figure in charge, boss or royalty

Knife: Someone may mean you harm or you have self-destructive tendencies.

Knight: rescuer- a knight in shining armor, someone to swoop in and save the day.

Ladder: Progress in spiritual or worldly status. Climbing the ladder of success.

Lake: water=emotion, a peaceful tranquil place to pour out emotion or quiet meditation

Letter: something important will be delivered. or a message from the Other Side

Library: a need for further knowledge, information. May refer to the Akashic records.

Light bulb: an idea, surrounded by the light-spirituality

Luggage: a trip or journey, if overflowing excess "baggage:" we need to eliminate.

Magician: clever or tricky, may represent knowledge from higher realms, mystical powers, making something from nothing.

Mirror: a time of reflection, self examination of what is going on in your life, relationships and values.

Money: wealth, may mean an increase as in a promotion, success of a business or an inheritance.

Moon: The moon has always been linked with fertility and may show personal growth. Associated with water, the growth may be emotional. Or travel overseas.

Mountains: An obstacle to overcome if you are at the bottom of one. an achievement if standing on the top of one!

Mouse: feeling inadequate, small or weak. not speaking up for one self as in quiet as a church mouse

Music: an ear for music, talent with musical instrument, enjoy listening to it. if specific song, who does it remind you of-may be communication from the Sprit World.

Ocean: deep emotions, may indicate a trip over the ocean.

Owl: Knowledge. You will gain greater wisdom. Higher learning indicated.

Path: The direction you are taking in life. Note any other symbols you may see on the path. Is it smooth and beautiful or rough and barren?

Peace sign: easy going, laid back, hippy. gentler times. a need to chill out and smell the flowers.

Pen: a writer, put ideas down on paper, get it in writing.

Pig: Are you being stubborn and "pig headed"? It is also a symbol of selfishness.

Pipe: may represent older man. a pipe smoker. I often will smell pipe smoke when I connect to those in the Spirit world who were pipe smokers here.

Policeman: Are you feeling guilty about something? Do you feel you need protection?

Puppet: feeling controlled by someone. Manipulated

Queen: Shows the motherly side of your nature or the guiding intuitive self. Your intuition will guide your future.

Radio: communication from Spirit perhaps in the lyrics.

Rain: cleansing of emotions, pour out your heart, or time to save for a rainy day

Rats: Aspects of yourself or others that probably frighten or disgust you. There could be problems ahead. (Rats backwards is Star)

Rope: something is tied together, connected or it may mean a person is troubled, at the end of their rope. If it is a noose Spirit has indicated to me they committed suicide

Rose: A symbol of love and a mystical symbol for enlightenment. You may see other flowers ask yourself what associations they have for you. My mother's and grandmother's name is Rose (Rose Mary) so I associate with a motherly figure whenever I see or hear the name rose.

Revolver: Do you feel angry about something. Or perhaps you will get another shot at an opportunity.

Sand: the beach, unstable ground, desert. It is my symbol for fun in the sun at the beach.

School: higher education, a need to learn new techniques

Scrolls: ancient wisdom, certificate of learning, degree

Shark: danger, ruthless clever behavior just below the surface

Smiley face: happy, or showing a happy face on the outside and inwardly unhappy.

Smoke: may indicate an actual fire. Things may be unclear, hazy wait till the smoke clears.

Snail: things moving slowly.

Stork: a baby is on its way

Storm: An inner conflict overwhelming you or trouble ahead.

Suitcase: travel plans, see baggage

Spider: You may distrust others. Be careful about entering formal agreements, you may get trapped.

Telephone: someone may reach out to you, especially someone you haven't heard from in a while

Third eye: Intuition, psychic phenomenon, a spiritual person. Clairvoyance , a person with second sight. the sixth chakra

Throat: communication, time to speak up. A person who is a speaker or singer. May also indicate something is wrong with thyroid. The fifth chakra

Train: The direction of your life at the moment. Be careful that you don't miss an opportunity.

Tree: Does the tree bear fruit? Is it strong like the oak or rotten, withered and battered? Trees are strong yet they can bend with the wind. Perhaps you should do the same when faced with adversity. Bend don't break!

Violence: If the images you see are of a violent theme then there may be a need for you to express your emotions in a natural, gentle way.

Wheel: an actual wheel may mean it is time to check your tires. May also represent wheel of fortune as in opportunities coming your way.

Zodiac: Astrological signs Aquarius, Pisces, Aries, Taurus, Gemini, Cancer, Leo, Virgo, Libra, Scorpio, Sagittarius, Capricorn each having different characteristics

Zoo Animals: You feel caged.
A great book I refer to all the time is *Animal Speak* by Ted Andrews. This book is wonderful for looking up the meanings of animals that cross your path. Pay attention to where and how frequently you see them. And in particular if you were thinking of a person or question just before you spotted them.

Dear Readers,

As I was writing this book I was "led" to write a fictional book which has wonderful characters that I hope you will fall in love with as much as I have. It has many twists and turns which will keep you intrigued as to how it will all turn out. The title says it all, "Ancient Lovers Never Forget".

Here are a few pages:

Ancient Lovers Never Forget

by Arlene Michel Rich

Do you remember the exact moment in time when your life changed dramatically because of a chance encounter. Actually, since I do not believe in co incidences it was Destiny we met on that hot July evening. I was the guest speaker at a woman's conference. Sharon my contact person had met me at the door of the hotel to walk me back to the room I would be presenting in. As she and I turned the corner there she was. My heart stood still. As we got closer Sharon introduced us. Logan reached out her hand looking me straight in the eyes and I was mesmerized by her hypnotic gaze. I reached out to shake her hand and with that Logan pulled me close and kissed me full on the lips with such passion that had she not been holding me so tightly I surely would have fallen over. As I felt her start to pull away I reached out with my tongue and found hers willingly. My heart felt as if it was going to fly from my chest. My lower regions were pulsing, each cell in my body had been awakened. After what seemed like an eternity I pulled away when I heard my host Sharon gasp. She exclaimed, "Well obviously you two know each other very well!"

Logan's eyes never left mine as she took a step to my side and said with a smirk on her face, "I've been waiting centuries to do that again, till next time!" As I stood there watching her leave I felt a part of my soul had been reawakened. Though I had not had the pleasure of meeting this beautiful woman before today, somewhere in the depths of my soul I knew her. As I watched her stride away with that sway of her blonde wavy shoulder length hair she turned giving me a final wink. It was like a shot of electricity was sent through the air straight to my heart. I swear I could hear an audible snap as it reached me.

A part of me wanted to run after her and just hold her in my arms. I had so many questions and if I didn't have hundreds of people in a hall waiting to hear me speak about ghosts and the

Paranormal I would have done just that. Logan's parting comment, "Till next time" gave me hope there would be a next time.

The next few hours flew by in a haze. I gave my lecture to a packed auditorium, stayed after to sign my books and answer questions and take numerous photos. I often think if I were to look at my eyes in one of those photos who would I see staring back? I know my mind was on Logan and how soon I could see her. How was I going to find her? She hadn't left me with any information at all. The only thing I did know was her kiss left me reeling and wanting more, oh much more!

I asked Sharon what Logan's last name was and how I could get in touch with her. Although she didn't ask any questions, she was clearly gob smacked that I didn't know it after she witnessed that arduous kiss. She said that Logan had approached her early in the day to make sure I would be presenting my lecture in that specific hall but she had only said her first name. Obviously there was no mistaking Logan was waiting for me and wanted to meet me before anyone else would get there. If I was an artist I could draw her picture it was now ingrained in my mind. She had been wearing a white frilly blouse that just gently hugged her shoulders. Her long brown skirt came mid-calf on her cream colored legs. She wore a long gold chain with an Egyptian ankh on it. I had noticed it when she shook my hand and drew me in. It gently popped out from between her ample bosom. I noticed she wore a gold band ring with a carnelian stone on her right hand. I hadn't noticed if she had anything on her left hand. But her smile when she winked at me was most mesmerizing with her beautiful hazel eyes and big dimples I could willingly drown in.

Sharon and some others who had set up this lecture wanted to take me to a late supper in a trendy Manhattan club but I really wasn't hungry for food. After some convincing I reluctantly agreed. A town car whisked us down fifth avenue to a trendy club in Soho. Of course Sharon had made the arrangements earlier so we didn't have to stand on that long roped off queue to get in. We were led into a cavernous secluded corner of the club. A band was playing and the music was familiar but not distinguishable with all the loud chatter of the other diners. I noticed the dark ornate oak bar had people three deep waiting to get a drink. It felt good to sit down and relax for a while and just notice my surroundings. Without ordering, a favorite drink of mine was placed in front of me. Glasses were raised and a toast was given on my behalf. As the night wore on and the music got louder I realized I had not told anyone what my favorite drink was. That was very curious. Just then as I was about to ask Sharon how she had found out what my old time favorite drink was, another one was placed in front of me. I knew I had never written about it before. I felt her presence before she leaned over and whispered in my ear, "I hope I remembered your drink correctly". As I turned my head in the direction of the whisper she kissed me. It was sweet with a need that was just below the surface. As she pulled away she said there was much more waiting for me if I wanted and I should meet her outside in twenty minutes. The whole exchange happened so quickly that I wasn't sure I hadn't dreamt it. No one at the table seemed to have noticed or if they did they were too polite to ask questions. Twenty minutes seemed like an eternity to have to wait.